STUDY GUIDE

Not Ashamed

Paul's Letter to the Romans

W. Robert Godfrey

LIGONIER MINISTRIES
Renew your Mind.
LIGONIER.ORG | 800-435-4343

421 Ligonier Court, Sanford, FL 32771
Email: info@ligonier.org

Printed in China.

Contents

Introduction

Many consider Paul's letter to the Romans to be his magnum opus. John Calvin believed that studying Romans unveils "the most hidden treasures of Scripture." In this teaching series, Dr. W. Robert Godfrey undertakes an exciting, verse-by-verse adventure through the book of Romans, giving us a glimpse at the heart of the Apostle and the heart of the gospel.

This study guide is a companion to the video teaching series. Whether you are using the DVDs, streaming the videos on Ligonier.org, or going through the course in Ligonier Connect, this resource is designed to help you make the most of the learning experience. For each message in the series, there is a corresponding lesson in this guide. Here is what you will find in each lesson:

INTRODUCTION	The introduction is a brief paragraph that summarizes the content covered in the lecture and considered in the study guide lesson. **How to use:** Use the introduction to each lesson to get a sense of the big picture before watching the video. Refer to these statements as you work through the study guide to remind you of what you have already covered and where you are headed.
LEARNING GOALS	The learning goals are the knowledge and skills that the study guide lesson will endeavor to equip you with as you work through the lecture content. **How to use:** Familiarize yourself with the goals of each lesson before engaging its contents. Keeping the overall purpose in mind as you watch each video and reflect on or discuss the questions will help you get the most out of each lesson.
KEY IDEAS	The key ideas are the major points or takeaways from the lecture. **How to use:** Use these ideas to prepare yourself for each lesson and to review previous lessons. They describe specifically the knowledge that each lecture is communicating.

REFLECTION & DISCUSSION QUESTIONS	The questions are the guided reflection and/or discussion component of the lesson that is intended to help you prepare for, process, and organize what you are learning. **How to use:** Reflect on individually or discuss in a group the questions in the order in which they appear in the lesson. The time stamps in the right margin indicate where the answers to questions during the video can be found.
PRAYER	The prayer section offers suggestions for how to close the lesson in prayer with respect to what was taught in the lecture. **How to use:** Consider using each lesson's prayer section as a guide to personal or group prayer. These sections follow the ACTS prayer model, which you can learn more about in R.C. Sproul's Crucial Questions booklet *Does Prayer Change Things?* This helpful guide is available as a free e-book at Ligonier.org.
REVIEW QUIZ	The review quiz is a set of six multiple-choice questions that appears at the end of each lesson. **How to use:** Use each quiz to check your comprehension and memory of the major points covered in each lecture. It will be most beneficial to your learning if you take a lesson's quiz either sometime between lessons or just before you begin the next lesson in the study guide.
ANSWER KEY	The answer key provides explanations for the reflection and discussion questions and answers to the multiple-choice questions in the review quiz. **How to use:** Use the answer key to check your own answers or when you do not know the answer. Note: Do not give in too quickly; struggling for a few moments to recall an answer reinforces it in your mind.

Study Schedules

The following table suggests four plans for working through the *Not Ashamed* video teaching series and this companion study guide. Whether you are going through this series on your own or with a group, these schedules should help you plan your study path.

	Extended 25-Week Plan	Standard 23-Week Plan	Abbreviated 12-Week Plan	Intensive 8-Week Plan
Week	**Lesson**			
1	*	1	1–2	1–3
2	1	2	3–4	4–6
3	2	3	5–6	7–9
4	3	4	7–8	10–12
5	4	5	9–10	13–15
6	5	6	11–12	16–18
7	6	7	13–14	19–21
8	7	8	15–16	22–23
9	8	9	17–18	
10	9	10	19–20	
11	10	11	21–22	
12	11	12	23	
13	12	13		
14	13	14		
15	14	15		
16	15	16		
17	16	17		
18	17	18		
19	18	19		

	Extended 25-Week Plan	Standard 23-Week Plan	Abbreviated 12-Week Plan	Intensive 8-Week Plan
Week	**Lesson**			
20	19	20		
21	20	21		
22	21	22		
23	22	23		
24	23			
25	*			

* For these weeks, rather than completing lessons, spend your time discussing and praying about your learning goals for the study (the first week) and the most valuable takeaways from the study (the last week).

1

Paul's Concerns

INTRODUCTION

Paul's epistle to the Romans has a special place in Scripture for its insights into the truth of the gospel of our Lord Jesus Christ. But this letter was not written in a vacuum. In this lesson, Dr. Godfrey introduces Paul's letter to the Romans by exploring Paul's reasons, which become clear after a close reading of the letter, for sitting down to write it.

LEARNING GOALS

When you have finished this lesson, you should be able to:

- Appreciate the theological majesty and pastoral scope of Paul's letter to the Romans
- Identify Paul's pastoral concerns that drive the theology of the letter
- Summarize the criticisms that the Apostle faced and addressed

KEY IDEAS

- Paul wrote his letter to the Romans with primarily pastoral concerns.
- Paul needed to defend his ministry and preaching of the gospel as the Apostle to the gentiles to the congregation in Rome, whom he had never met but planned to visit soon.
- Paul addresses charges about his teaching that relate to how boldly he preached the gospel of grace; opponents accused him of promoting lawlessness and forgetting Israel's place in redemptive history, for example.

REFLECTION & DISCUSSION QUESTIONS

Before the Video

What Do You Think?

Take a moment to answer the following questions. They will prepare you for the lecture.

- Why are you undertaking this study through Romans?
- Drawing from your prior knowledge of the letter, what is Paul's main purpose in writing it?

Scripture Reading

And thus I make it my ambition to preach the gospel, not where Christ has already been named, lest I build on someone else's foundation, but as it is written, "Those who have never been told of him will see, and those who have never heard will understand." This is the reason why I have so often been hindered from coming to you. But now, since I no longer have any room for work in these regions, and since I have longed for many years to come to you, I hope to see you in passing as I go to Spain, and to be helped on my journey there by you, once I have enjoyed your company for a while.

—Romans 15:20–24

- Why had Paul not yet visited Rome before writing his letter? What is the reason that he wanted to go to Rome?

During the Video

Answer the following questions while you watch the video. They will guide you through the lecture.

Paul's Approach *0:00–10:48*

- What is a common misconception about Paul's letter to the Romans?
- What is an important question that we ought to ask when studying Romans?
- Why are Paul's pastoral concerns not as apparent in his letter to the Romans than in other letters?

Paul's Motivations *10:48–24:43*

- What important lesson does Paul teach us in Romans through his use of Scripture?

- What are some of the criticisms that motivated Paul to write his letter?

After the Video

Answer the following questions after you have finished the lecture. They will help you identify and summarize the major points.

- "For I am not ashamed of the gospel" (Rom. 1:16). Have you ever wondered why Paul said this? How does Dr. Godfrey's approach help illumine why Paul said it?

  If you are in a group, have the members discuss how they have approached Paul's letter to the Romans in the past, perhaps as if it were a systematic theology. Ask: What makes Romans so compelling to read and study?

- Why might Paul have been accused of ignoring the place of the Israelites in redemptive history or of neglecting the value and power of the law in the Christian life? How did he respond to such accusations?

  If you are in a group, have the members identify and discuss why it does not make sense for Christians to set aside the law entirely, even though it cannot justify.

- Which of the accusations that Paul faced do you consider to be the most formidable? Which one did Dr. Godfrey say was probably the Romans' most fundamental concern?

  If you are in a group, have the members identify a time when someone has misinterpreted their beliefs. Ask: Why is it sometimes difficult to convey the truth about God's free grace to people?

PRAYER

Commit what you have learned from God's Word in this lesson to prayer.

- Praise God for His Word to us, both in Scripture and in Christ.
- Confess the areas where you might be questioning fellow Christians' motives or beliefs in a way that is similar to that of Paul's accusers.

- Thank God for granting you a salvation that is not made secure through your obedience to the law.
- Ask God to bless your study of Romans with personal spiritual insight.

REVIEW QUIZ

Use these multiple-choice questions to measure what you learned from this lesson.

1. A commentary on the book of Romans was the first Bible commentary written by which of the following?
   a. Philip Melanchthon
   b. Martin Luther
   c. Martin Bucer
   d. John Calvin

2. Paul explicitly states his reasons and pastoral concerns in writing his letter to the Romans.
   a. True
   b. False

3. Which one of the following was *not* an accusation that Paul likely faced?
   a. That Paul's teachings were dangerous.
   b. That Paul's teachings promoted lawlessness.
   c. That Paul's teachings were fruitless among the gentiles.
   d. That Paul's teachings neglected the place of Israel in redemptive history.

4. How many times does Paul quote from the Old Testament in his letter to the Romans?
   a. Fewer than twenty times
   b. Fewer than fifty times
   c. More than seventy times
   d. More than ninety times

5. Paul taught the advantage of the Jews as having another way of salvation.
   a. True
   b. False

6. Which one of the following passages does *not* relate to Paul's defense of his ministry to the Romans?
   a. "For I am not ashamed of the gospel" (Rom. 1:16).
   b. "Then what advantage has the Jew?" (Rom. 3:1).
   c. "Are we to continue in sin that grace may abound?" (Rom. 6:1).
   d. "Present your bodies as a living sacrifice" (Rom. 12:1).

Answer Key—Paul's Concerns

REFLECTION & DISCUSSION QUESTIONS

Before the Video

What Do You Think?

These are personal questions. The answers should be based on your own knowledge and experience.

Scripture Reading

- Why had Paul not yet visited Rome before writing his letter? What is the reason that he wanted to go to Rome?

  Paul was the Apostle to the gentiles. He had a heart to reach those among the nations who had never heard about Jesus Christ. Though Rome had many gentiles among its congregation, Paul had not visited the church because it had already been established. He desired to see others won to Christ elsewhere, which is precisely why he wanted to go to Rome after his letter, to have a place from which to reach Spain for the sake of the gospel.

During the Video

Paul's Approach

- What is a common misconception about Paul's letter to the Romans?

  Many people think of Romans as a comprehensive systematic theology. On the one hand, it richly presents the doctrines of grace, but on the other hand, it is a letter that was written with a purpose to particular people. Paul had pressing pastoral concerns, so the letter isn't merely theological.

- What is an important question that we ought to ask when studying Romans?

  Because we can lose sight of the pastoral issues behind Paul's letter, we ought to ask why *Paul is writing instead of solely focusing on* what *he is writing. In this manner, we can connect the theology of Romans to Paul's intentions, which will in turn give us greater insight into its theology.*

- Why are Paul's pastoral concerns not as apparent in his letter to the Romans than in other letters?

  In other letters, Paul is explicit about the issues he is addressing, at times even quoting correspondence back to his recipients, as in his letters to the Corinthians. Paul had never been to Rome, however. Though he knew some people in the congregation, the congregation as a whole did not personally know him. The church in Rome had doubts about Paul and his teaching, and he addressed those doubts boldly throughout the letter, though not always explicitly.

Paul's Motivations

- What important lesson does Paul teach us in Romans through his use of Scripture?

  Throughout his letter, Paul quotes from the Old Testament more than seventy times, and from this, an important lesson emerges for us: how to read the Old Testament. Paul gives us a theology of the Old Testament that clues us in on how to read it ourselves, giving us insights into the history of redemption and the role of the law in the Christian life.

- What are some of the criticisms that motivated Paul to write his letter?

  When reading between the lines of Paul's letters, one can discern the criticism that Paul was addressing. Paul's critics said that his teaching was dangerous, and they also believed that he had forgotten a number of things, including the special place of Israel in God's economy and the value of God's law. His critics even accused him of promoting sin as a means of increasing one's grace. All these false accusations were provided as reasons to the Christians in Rome for Paul's failure to visit them.

After the Video

- "For I am not ashamed of the gospel" (Rom. 1:16). Have you ever wondered why Paul said this? How does Dr. Godfrey's approach help illumine why Paul said it?

  Apart from understanding the pastoral context and intents of Paul's letter, this idea of being ashamed of the gospel may strike some as strange at first glance. Dr. Godfrey intends for us to see the reasons that Paul is writing his letter, and one of the accusations that he may have been facing or a doubt lingering in the minds of the Romans was that Paul was too ashamed of his teaching to visit the congregation. But in saying that he is not ashamed, Paul is declaring with boldness the nature of the gospel that is received only by faith for Israel and the nations, regardless of how some may have misinterpreted him.

- Why might Paul have been accused of ignoring the place of the Israelites in redemptive history or of neglecting the value and power of the law in the Christian life? How did he respond to such accusations?

  Paul stressed that the law cannot save anyone and that salvation is only through faith in Jesus Christ for both the Israelites and the nations. Paul was indeed called to be the Apostle to the gentiles. It would have been easy to accuse him of forgetting his heritage by the very nature of that mission, and because he spoke against the law's power to save, it would have been easy to conclude from his teaching that the law had no value for him. But Paul did not believe this, and throughout his letter he demonstrated with the Old Testament that the law was never intended to be used as a means of salvation and that God's plans for the nations had long been prophesied.

- Which of the accusations that Paul faced do you consider to be the most formidable? Which one did Dr. Godfrey say was probably the Romans' most fundamental concern?

  The answer to the first question takes into consideration all the accusations to determine which one you consider to be most challenging for Paul to surmount. Dr. Godfrey said that probably the most fundamental concern of the Romans was the charge that Paul promoted sin so that grace might abound (see Rom. 6:1–2). This charge is related to the accusation that he had forgotten the place of the law in the Christian life, but it goes even further to suggest that Paul endorsed absolute lawlessness.

REVIEW QUIZ

1. **D.**
   Although Bucer and Melanchthon had already published commentaries on the book of Romans, Calvin believed that a shorter commentary on Romans would serve the church excellently. Additionally, Romans is a significant and profound book of the Bible, but Calvin bravely decided to write his first commentary on it.

2. **B.**
   One the reasons why people might be surprised by Dr. Godfrey's calling Romans a "pastoral" letter is that Paul's pastoral concerns in writing the letter are easily overlooked. He states them not explicitly but implicitly in his overall argument of the letter.

3. **C.**
   While Paul faced many accusations, that his ministry and teaching among the gentiles was fruitless could not be one of them. As the Apostle to the gentiles, Paul had his work among the nations used by God to great effect.

4. **C.**
   Paul's use of the Old Testament in his letter to the Romans could be understood as a lesson in biblical interpretation to that congregation. Paul quotes from the Old Testament more than seventy times to defend his gospel to the Romans.

5. **B.**
   One of Paul's teachings in line with the gospel of Jesus Christ was that the law equally condemned both the Israelites and the nations, and so keeping the law was unable to save anyone. Paul taught that both Jews and gentiles had the same need for salvation, and both had to receive it the same way—by faith.

6. **D.**
   Paul was maligned concerning his willingness to visit Rome, but he declared that he was not ashamed of the gospel. Paul was accused of forgetting about the special place of the Israelites in the history of redemption, but he consistently pointed to their advantages that were by God's grace. Paul was also accused of teaching law-

lessness, but he rejected the idea that grace gives someone permission to sin. Paul's call to present our bodies as living sacrifices is consistent with such teaching but does not reveal his concerns to defend his ministry to the Romans.

2

The Shape & Opening of the Letter

INTRODUCTION

Paul's style throughout Romans can make us question why Paul deals with certain topics or even what he means. Knowing Paul's pastoral concerns helps us with this, but so does understanding the overall structure of his letter. In this lesson, Dr. Godfrey addresses questions about Paul's clarity and provides his helpful outline of Paul's letter, concluding his lecture where Paul begins: his self-introduction as the servant Apostle of the long-awaited Lord Jesus Christ.

LEARNING GOALS

When you have finished this lesson, you should be able to:

- Understand Paul's manner of writing
- Provide a summary outline of Paul's letter
- Explain important phrases in Paul's introduction

KEY IDEAS

- Paul's style in Romans fits his pastoral concerns in writing the letter.
- Romans is organized as a chiasm, focusing attention at the center of the letter.
- Paul's introduction in his letter to the Romans is longer than his introduction in every other letter and contains Paul's understanding of who he is and who Jesus is.

REFLECTION & DISCUSSION QUESTIONS

Before the Video

What Do You Think?

Take a moment to answer the following questions. They will prepare you for the lecture.

- When you're meeting someone for the first time, what do you tell that person about yourself?

- Why is understanding the Old Testament important for understanding the New Testament?

Scripture Reading

Paul, called by the will of God to be an apostle of Christ Jesus, and our brother Sosthenes, to the church of God that is in Corinth, to those sanctified in Christ Jesus, called to be saints together with all those who in every place call upon the name of our Lord Jesus Christ, both their Lord and ours: Grace to you and peace from God our Father and the Lord Jesus Christ.

—1 Corinthians 1:1–3

- What are the parts of Paul's greetings, as in this example from his first letter to the Corinthians?

During the Video

Answer the following questions while you watch the video. They will guide you through the lecture.

Style *0:00–5:44*

- What is the tone of Paul's letter to the Romans?

- What might Paul be trying to accomplish with the manner in which he writes in difficult sections of his letter? Where does Paul strive to be particularly clear?

Organization *5:44–11:54*

- What are the main sections of Dr. Godfrey's outline?

Introduction *11:54–25:00*

- What is unique about Paul's greeting to the Romans?

- How does Paul understand his identity and role as an Apostle? Where does he root his understanding of his identity and that of Jesus Christ?

After the Video

Answer the following questions after you have finished the lecture. They will help you identify and summarize the major points.

- What stands out to you most about Paul's introduction to his letter to the Romans?

  If you are in a group, have the members discuss their answers to this question. Then ask: How does Paul's first self-identification as a slave before an Apostle help you think about your Christian life?

- How does Paul's understanding of the Old Testament emerge in his introduction? Why is the Old Testament important for our understanding of who Jesus Christ is?

  If you are in a group, have the members come up with a list of several concepts that are central to the Christian worldview and that would be hard to understand without knowledge of the Old Testament. Ask: What gaps of knowledge do we have to fill for unbelievers when we share the gospel?

- What is the center point of Paul's letter? Why might this be significant?

  If you are in a group, have the members identify and discuss how the truth of the gospel has changed the way they think, feel, and act.

PRAYER

Commit what you have learned from God's Word in this lesson to prayer.

- Praise God for His providential and sovereign hand over history to bring about His will.
- Confess areas in your life in which you struggle to live in service to Jesus Christ.
- Thank God for having set you apart for service to Christ and His gospel.
- Ask God to help you to walk in greater measures of obedience by the Spirit.

REVIEW QUIZ

Use these multiple-choice questions to measure what you learned from this lesson.

1. Paul is just as clear and simple in every other place in Romans as he is in his presentation of the gospel throughout the letter.
   a. True
   b. False
2. Paul's style in his letter to the Romans may have been used to do which one of the following?
   a. Confuse the Romans for their entertaining rumors about him
   b. Commend the Romans for their sophistication and erudition
   c. Slow the Romans down to consider complex issues
   d. Elicit sympathy from the Romans because of his delayed visit
3. Which section of Paul's letter is at the center of its chiastic structure?
   a. "Salvation Needed"
   b. "Salvation Provided"
   c. "Salvation Experienced"
   d. "Salvation Lived Out"
4. What are the first words of Romans?
   a. "Jesus Christ"
   b. "Paul, an apostle"
   c. "Paul, a servant"
   d. "Set apart"
5. In his introduction, Paul begins to communicate his view of the Old Testament as preparatory for Jesus Christ and His continued mission through the church.
   a. True
   b. False
6. Which phrase poses difficulty for commentators to interpret in Paul's introduction?
   a. "According to the flesh"
   b. "Declared to be the Son of God"
   c. "The obedience of faith"
   d. "The Spirit of holiness"

Answer Key—The Shape & Opening of the Letter

REFLECTION & DISCUSSION QUESTIONS

Before the Video

What Do You Think?

These are personal questions. The answers should be based on your own knowledge and experience.

Scripture Reading

- What are the parts of Paul's greetings, as in this example from his first letter to the Corinthians?

  In Paul's greetings, exemplified here in his introduction to his first letter to the Corinthians, Paul begins by identifying himself. He then identifies the recipients of his letter. Finally, he pronounces an Apostolic blessing on his recipients.

During the Video

Style

- What is the tone of Paul's letter to the Romans?

  Unlike in Paul's letter to the Galatians, where his tone is overtly confrontational, Paul's tone in his letter to the Romans is gentle. In his letter to the Galatians, Paul needed to address major issues that were jeopardizing the gospel, but his gentle tone in writing to the Romans demonstrates his awareness that the Roman Christians needed an adjustment and not a confrontation.

- What might Paul be trying to accomplish with the manner in which he writes in difficult sections of his letter? Where does Paul strive to be particularly clear?

  At times in Romans, Paul's style is complex and can be confusing. Scholars even struggle to understand Romans because of Paul's style, whether he is being argumentatively complex, repetitive, or hyperbolic. Perhaps Paul was attempting to slow the Romans down and cause them to think about complex issues. This would be to show them that he knows what he is talking about. Yet despite his complexity, Paul is crystal clear when it comes to the truth of the gospel, which he teaches plainly so that it will not be lost on anyone.

Organization

- What are the main sections of Dr. Godfrey's outline?

  The sections of Dr. Godfrey's outline for Romans are as follows:

  1. *Introduction (1:1–17)*
  2. *Salvation Needed (1:18–3:20)*
  3. *Salvation Provided (3:21–5:21)*
  4. *Salvation Experienced (6:1–8:39)*
  5. *Salvation Assured (9:1–11:36)*
  6. *Salvation Lived Out (12:1–15:7)*
  7. *Conclusion (15:8–16:27)*

Introduction

- What is unique about Paul's greeting to the Romans?

  In nearly all his letters, Paul identifies himself, identifies his recipients, and pronounces a blessing on his recipients before getting into the heart of his writing. In eight of Paul's letters, this introductory material is only two verses long. In his letter to the Romans, this material is seven verses long, so even though it follows the same general formula as his other letters, it is unique in terms of its length.

- How does Paul understand his identity and role as an Apostle? Where does he root his understanding of his identity and that of Jesus Christ?

  Paul first introduces himself as a servant of Jesus Christ, and this is important because he sees his role as an Apostle as one of obedience and service. Being an Apostle was not a self-appointment; Paul was called to it by Jesus Christ, particularly to be an Apostle to the nations. That the nations would be called to faith was something long foreseen in the Old Testament, where Paul draws on the concept to frame his calling as someone "set apart," just as people and instruments of worship were set apart for temple service. Paul also roots his understanding of Jesus Christ in the Old Testament, particularly in identifying Him as the Son of David.

After the Video

- What stands out to you most about Paul's introduction to his letter to the Romans?

  The answers to this question may vary but should take into consideration how Paul's introduction to the Romans is packed with significance. It contains a standard greeting wherein Paul identifies himself, identifies his recipients, and pronounces a blessing on his recipients, but his self-identification alone spans six of the seven verses in this introduction. In it, Paul identifies himself as an Apostle-slave of Jesus Christ while unfolding his understanding of who Jesus is and of his service to Him for the sake of the nations.

- How does Paul's understanding of the Old Testament emerge in his introduction? Why is the Old Testament important for our understanding of who Jesus Christ is?

  Paul shows that he understands himself in Old Testament categories when he calls himself "set apart" (Rom. 1:1), but he also conveys his understanding of the forward-looking nature of the New Testament in his introduction. He was "set apart" for the gospel of God that was "promised beforehand through his prophets in the holy Scriptures" (v. 2). Throughout Romans, Paul is going to show how the gospel as expressed through the doctrine of justification by faith and as going forth to the nations had long been declared in Scripture. This gospel is ultimately about Jesus Christ, who is described in connection with the Old Testament—namely, in linking Him to David. His very title Christ *can be understood only in light of the Old Testament, for He is the "Anointed One," the long-awaited Messiah. The Old Testament provides us with this conceptual category and others that are related to Jesus, such as His offices of Prophet, Priest, and King.*

- What is the center point of Paul's letter? Why might this be significant?

  Whereas answers to the second question may vary, Dr. Godfrey presented the idea that Romans has a chiastic structure, and chiasms stress the material at their center. At the center of the chiasm in Romans is chapters 6–8, which largely deal with the new life of the Christian as lived out in the freedom of Christ by the Spirit.

REVIEW QUIZ

1. **B.**
   Many scholars have been puzzled by Paul's style and line of argument at various points in his letter to the Romans. That being said, Paul's writing is marked by clarity and simplicity when it comes to the basics of the gospel.

2. **C.**
   Paul did not set out to intentionally confuse the Romans. Neither did he set out to give room for boasting among the Romans on account of their intelligence, nor to give credence to any false rumors about the reasons for his delay. Rather, Paul wrote in a complex style at times to slow the Romans down and thus help them digest complex issues.

3. **C.**
   Romans displays some features of a chiasm, a literary structure that allows one to focus on the center of the letter for a point of emphasis. Dr. Godfrey titled the center section of Paul's letter "Salvation Experienced," which covers chapters 6–8.

4. **C.**
   The first two words of the Greek in Paul's letter to the Romans are Paulos doulos, *which means "Paul, a servant" or "Paul, a slave." Before Paul introduces himself as an Apostle or even the One who sent him, he introduces himself as a slave of Jesus Christ.*

5. **A.**
Paul immediately appeals to the Old Testament to tell the Romans about who Jesus is. Although he does not quote from the Old Testament, he does display his interpretive grid for understanding the Old Testament not as a document that was an end in itself but as something that always looked forward to its fulfillment in Christ and the gospel's going forth to every nation.

6. **C.**
While each of these phrases, as with all Scripture, needs to be interpreted with care, the phrase "the obedience of faith" (Rom. 1:5) has been particularly challenging for commentators. Dr. Godfrey pointed to the amount of space given to the interpretation of this phrase in commentaries as evidence for this.

3

The Power of God for Salvation

INTRODUCTION

God saves sinners through His preached Word. Paul understood and boldly proclaimed this to the Christians in Rome, that the gospel is "the power of God for salvation to everyone who believes" (Rom. 1:16). In this lesson, Dr. Godfrey continues through Paul's introduction to his letter and challenges ancient and modern interpretations of Paul's teaching in Romans 1.

LEARNING GOALS

When you have finished this lesson, you should be able to:

- Appreciate the significance of Paul's opening phrase despite our familiarity with it
- Defend Paul's Apostolic interpretation of Habakkuk as support for his position that salvation is by faith alone
- Weigh the historical evidence regarding the Apostle Peter's role at the church in Rome

KEY IDEAS

- Paul opens his letter with a sincere appreciation for the Christians in Rome and a desire to bless them with the grace and peace that flow from the gospel.
- God exercises His power through the preaching of the gospel.
- The Apostolic reading and use of the Old Testament is true and reliable.
- The Roman Catholic belief that the Apostle Peter was the first bishop of Rome is not supported by first-century historical evidence.

REFLECTION & DISCUSSION QUESTIONS

Before the Video

What Do You Think?

Take a moment to answer the following questions. They will prepare you for the lecture.

- Why is it important for you to regularly attend worship? What role does the preached Word of God play in your Christian life?
- Why is it important to maintain that salvation is by grace alone through faith alone?

Scripture Reading

But since we were torn away from you, brothers, for a short time, in person not in heart, we endeavored the more eagerly and with great desire to see you face to face, because we wanted to come to you—I, Paul, again and again—but Satan hindered us. For what is our hope or joy or crown of boasting before our Lord Jesus at his coming? Is it not you? For you are our glory and joy.

—1 Thessalonians 2:17–20

- What phrases characterize Paul's heart for the churches that he served in this example?

During the Video

Answer the following questions while you watch the video. They will guide you through the lecture.

Paul's Heart for the Romans *0:00–6:45*

- In naming the recipients of his letter, what is Paul calling the Romans to?
- What might Paul's appreciation for the Romans indicate?

Paul and Habakkuk *6:45–16:30*

- Why does Paul mention both "Jew" and "Greek" in Romans 1:16?

- Why does Paul quote Habakkuk in Romans 1:17?

- How do proponents of the New Perspective on Paul interpret Paul's quotation of Habakkuk 2:4?

Where Is Peter? *16:30–24:07*

- What does Paul's silence about Peter in his letter to the Romans suggest?

- Even if Peter could be proved to have ties to the church in Rome historically, would that support the claims of the Roman Catholic Church?

After the Video

Answer the following questions after you have finished the lecture. They will help you identify and summarize the major points.

- We tend to pass by what may seem to be repetitive language in Scripture, but why ought we to slow down and consider such phrases as "grace and peace" in Paul's introduction to the Romans?

  If you are in a group, have the members each go to a different letter of the Apostle Paul and identify what's similar or different in the Apostolic blessings in the openings of his letters.
- How does the idea that salvation is through faith plus obedience challenge the gospel?

  If you are in a group, have the members describe how they remain humble as Christians, not seeing their good works or obedience as a reason to boast. Ask: Where does obedience fit into the Christian life, and why is it necessary?
- How can Romans, Peter's letters, and tradition all fit together to argue against the idea that Peter was the first bishop of Rome?

  If you are in a group, have the members discuss the Roman Catholic Church's claim that the pope does not err in the church's decrees. Ask: Does Scripture challenge this idea? Does history?

PRAYER

Commit what you have learned from God's Word in this lesson to prayer.

- Praise God for His loving nature as seen in His sending His Son so that we might have grace and peace.
- Confess areas in your life in which you are prone to harbor pride over any perceived goodness.
- Thank God for His protection of the church through the centuries even through periods of great error.
- Ask God to enrich your sense of awe at His free grace in Jesus Christ.

REVIEW QUIZ

Use these multiple-choice questions to measure what you learned from this lesson.

1. What does Paul commend the church in Rome for?
   a. Prayerfulness
   b. Obedience
   c. Generosity
   d. Faith
2. When Paul blesses the Romans with "grace . . . and peace" (Rom. 1:7), he is stressing the objective, not the subjective, aspect of peace with God.
   a. True
   b. False
3. What is the context of Habakkuk 2:4?
   a. Israel needs right worship, or it will meet judgment.
   b. Israel is realizing the promises that God will be worshiped universally.
   c. The righteous are living by an obedience that sets them apart in suffering.
   d. The righteous are living by faith in a promise that is yet to be fulfilled.
4. Which book of the Bible most suggests that Peter was in Rome before his death?
   a. Acts
   b. Romans
   c. 1 Peter
   d. 2 Peter
5. If the Apostle Peter can be established as the first bishop of Rome, Roman Catholic teaching concerning the papacy should be endorsed.
   a. True
   b. False

6. Which of the following is *not* at odds with Paul's teaching in Romans 1?
    a. Paul's first-century critics
    b. Roman Catholicism
    c. The New Perspective on Paul
    d. The Old Testament and Habakkuk

Answer Key—The Power of God for Salvation

REFLECTION & DISCUSSION QUESTIONS

Before the Video

What Do You Think?

These are personal questions. The answers should be based on your own knowledge and experience.

Scripture Reading

- What phrases characterize Paul's heart for the churches that he served in this example?

  Though Paul's relationship with every church that he served was unique, Paul consistently displayed a longing to be with these churches in his letters. In this letter to the Thessalonians, he used phrases such as "more eagerly" and "great desire," even describing these Christians as his "hope," "joy," and "crown." As you will see in this lesson, Paul conveys this same heartfelt desire and appreciation to the Romans, despite not having yet visited the church.

During the Video

Paul's Heart for the Romans

- In naming the recipients of his letter, what is Paul calling the Romans to?

  In his introduction, Paul writes, "To all those in Rome who are loved by God and called to be saints" (Rom. 1:7). In identifying the Romans, Paul calls them to be what they are—saints. While the connection between the word saint *and the word* holiness *is lost in English, it is plain in the Greek. Paul is calling the Romans to holiness.*

- What might Paul's appreciation for the Romans indicate?

  Paul's appreciation and commendation of the Romans, although he has things to correct them on, indicate that Paul does not consider the criticism that has been mounted against him to be so severe that he takes great offense. It may also be the case that not the entire congregation is caught up in the false speculation against Paul. Perhaps it had infected only some of the congregation.

Paul and Habakkuk

- Why does Paul mention both "Jew" and "Greek" in Romans 1:16?

  Paul proclaims, "I am not ashamed of the gospel, for it is the power of God for salvation to everyone *who believes" (emphasis added). Paul mentions both Jew and*

Greek because God's plan for salvation is not different for either one. Everyone is saved through faith in Jesus Christ.

- Why does Paul quote Habakkuk in Romans 1:17?

  Paul's true conviction is that salvation through faith was always God's plan for His people. In quoting from Habakkuk 2:4, Paul is substantiating this claim. Paul is attempting to demonstrate in quoting the Old Testament at this point that his teaching is not a novel idea but something steeped in Scripture.

- How do proponents of the New Perspective on Paul interpret Paul's quotation of Habakkuk 2:4?

  Proponents of the New Perspective on Paul believe that Paul is not teaching justification by faith alone by quoting Habakkuk 2:4, which is how Luther understood Paul. Rather, they interpret Paul to mean that the just live by faithfulness*—namely, through faith plus obedience. This reading, however, is not consistent with the message of Romans as a whole.*

Where Is Peter?

- What does Paul's silence about Peter in his letter to the Romans suggest?

  The great historic claim of the Roman Catholic Church is that the Apostle Peter was the first bishop of Rome and that there is a continuation of the Apostolic ministry through the succession of bishops after him. An issue that is related to this claim is Peter's historical connection to the church in Rome. Paul does not mention Peter in his letter to the Romans, which was likely written in AD 57—thus suggesting that Peter was not in authority over the church or churches in Rome.

- Even if Peter could be proved to have ties to the church in Rome historically, would that support the claims of the Roman Catholic Church?

  The historical evidence related to Peter and his relationship with the church in Rome as its first bishop cannot be supported by Scripture. Though there is a very ancient account that Peter was martyred in Rome, many details in Scripture suggest that Peter was not in Rome for any significant time before his death. Even if we could prove that Peter was serving in Rome in this capacity, this would not support the Roman Catholic claim of papal infallibility, and many teachings of Rome work against such a bold claim.

After the Video

- We tend to pass by what may seem to be repetitive language in Scripture, but why ought we to slow down and consider such phrases as "grace and peace" in Paul's introduction to the Romans?

  One way of interpreting repeated words or phrases is to consider them redundant. Another interpretation is that they are important. Paul's greetings often contain the phrase "grace and peace." These are more than nice words or sentiments. For

Paul, grace and peace are realities that are brought about by the gospel. Grace is at the heart of our justification by faith (see Rom. 3:23–24). Likewise, peace is what we have with God through the gospel. If we pass over these words without reflecting on them, we lose the rich reminder that they provide.

- How does the idea that salvation is through faith plus obedience challenge the gospel?

  Proponents of the New Perspective on Paul deny that he teaches that salvation is by faith alone in such places as Romans 1:17, where he quotes Habakkuk 2:4. Rather, they believe Paul to be teaching that we are saved through faithfulness, which is faith plus obedience. This overturns the traditional reading of Romans because it overturns the gospel. The gospel is good news because our works are not factored into the equation. Otherwise, we could never be saved. Our salvation is by faith alone, and even our faith is by grace (see Eph. 2:8–10).

- How can Romans, Peter's letters, and tradition all fit together to argue against the idea that Peter was the first bishop of Rome?

  Tradition states that Peter died a martyr's death in Rome around AD 68–69. The Roman Catholic Church claims that he was the first bishop of Rome, but there is not enough evidence to support conclusively that Peter was in Rome for any extended period before his attested death. Paul wrote his letter in AD 57, but he did not mention Peter. In his first letter (written in AD 65), Peter alludes to Rome by the name of "Babylon," sending greetings from the city, but he does not say that he is sending these greetings from there. Finally, Peter does not mention Rome at all in his second letter, which was written in AD 67 or 68. All these details suggest that Peter might not have functioned in this role in the manner that is argued by the Roman Catholic Church.

REVIEW QUIZ

1. **D.**
   Perhaps ironically, Paul commends the Romans for their faith that is "proclaimed in all the world" (Rom. 1:8). Though he is certainly sincere, the rumors that were being spread about Paul connect to his stress on faith alone, yet the Romans, too, are known by their faith.

2. **B.**
   It is difficult to conclude that Paul would have only the objective aspect of peace in mind—namely, that we have peace with God and are no longer subject to His wrath because of Christ. Dr. Godfrey suggested that Paul had this objective aspect of peace on his mind as well as peace in a subjective sense, which is the peace that each of us feels individually when reflecting on gospel realities.

3. **D.**
Though Habakkuk speaks judgment on Israel for its sin, his prophecy is full of anticipation and hope even in the face of what will be Israel's suffering. Habakkuk provides a call to Israel during this time, that the righteous must rest in faith in God's deliverance, not losing hope or resting in their own righteousness.

4. **C.**
Near the end of his first letter, Peter writes, "She who is at Babylon, who is likewise chosen, sends you greetings" (1 Peter 5:13). Scholars believe that "Babylon" refers to Rome, so of all the evidence, this most strongly suggests that Peter was in Rome, though it is not conclusive. Remember, Peter does not state that he was also in Rome, and he does not mention Rome in his second letter.

5. **B.**
There is more to Roman Catholic doctrine than the claim that Peter was the first bishop of Rome. In addition to this claim, the church believes the popes are infallible when they make pronouncements. Even if Peter were established to be the first bishop of Rome, there is no support for such a claim, and there are reasons to doubt the historical accuracy of even the claim that Peter was Rome's first bishop.

6. **D.**
Proponents of the New Perspective on Paul interpret Paul's use of Habakkuk in much the same way that his first-century critics would have wished Paul to be using Habakkuk: to teach that salvation is not through faith alone. This is a Roman Catholic conviction, and one for which it has pronounced anathemas on Protestants. Paul was not, however, out of accord with the teaching of Scripture, and he endeavors throughout Romans to show his consistency with it.

4

The Seriousness of Sin

INTRODUCTION

God takes all sin seriously because He is holy. He is the Creator of all things, and the truth about Him is made plain in the things that have been made, yet people suppress this truth in the unrighteousness of idolatry and immorality. In this lesson, Dr. Godfrey explains how Paul's emphasis on the seriousness of sin against a holy God fits within his argument that salvation is desperately needed.

LEARNING GOALS

When you have finished this lesson, you should be able to:

- Trace Paul's argument in Romans 1:18–32 about the seriousness of sin
- Consider the unnaturalness of death and its place as a reminder of sin's penalty

KEY IDEAS

- Romans 1:18–3:20 can be understood as a complete literary unit and be called "Salvation Needed."
- All human beings have access to the truth about God and are without excuse for the suppression of this truth that leads to idolatry and immorality.
- We cannot understand God's anger against sin unless we understand His holiness.
- Death is a testimony that we live in a world where sin is so serious that death is its punishment.

REFLECTION & DISCUSSION QUESTIONS

Before the Video

What Do You Think?

Take a moment to answer the following questions. They will prepare you for the lecture.

- Are there certain sins that you tend to excuse yourself for committing?

- Do you think about death? How do you process these thoughts when they come up?

Scripture Reading

Therefore God gave them up in the lusts of their hearts to impurity, to the dishonoring of their bodies among themselves, because they exchanged the truth about God for a lie and worshiped and served the creature rather than the Creator, who is blessed forever! Amen.

—Romans 1:24–25

- What is God's response to idolatry?

During the Video

Answer the following questions while you watch the video. They will guide you through the lecture.

Idolatry and Immorality *0:00–15:36*

- What do we need to keep in mind when tracing Paul's arguments in Romans?

- What category within systematic theology is Paul employing in his argument in Romans 1? Define this category.

- What do we see Paul modeling his argument that idolatry leads to immorality on?

"Little" Sins *15:36–24:32*

- What misconception do we need to resist when considering Paul's list of sins in Romans 1?

- What might be Paul's intention for us in listing all these sins?

After the Video

Answer the following questions after you have finished the lecture. They will help you identify and summarize the major points.

- Is it unjust for God to judge people who have not heard the gospel? Why or why not?

  If you are in a group, have the members discuss what part of God's created order strikes them as the clearest evidence of His existence, power, and divine nature.

- Why does Paul bring up homosexuality in Romans 1? How is the veracity of Paul's argument in Romans 1 proved by recent LGBTQ activism?

  If you are in a group, have the members discuss how sins related to sexuality and gender seem to most challenge the spread of Christian ideas in public arenas. Ask: Why are these issues so at odds with the Christian worldview?

- How is the reality of death handled in your family? Is it treated as a natural part of life or referred to in "polite" terms? How might Romans 1 equip you to talk about these things with your family?

  If you are in a group, have the members share some difficult or encouraging experiences that they have had at funerals of loved ones. Ask: Why are moments like these great opportunities for the gospel?

PRAYER

Commit what you have learned from God's Word in this lesson to prayer.

- Praise God for His power and divine nature as revealed in creation.
- Confess ways that you have minimized or excused certain sins in your life.
- Thank God that He does not tolerate sin in His holiness and that He has dealt with it in His mercy to you in Christ.
- Ask God to grant you deeper conviction of sin and comfort of forgiveness through the Holy Spirit.

REVIEW QUIZ

Use these multiple-choice questions to measure what you learned from this lesson.

1. What conclusion must we keep in mind as we read Paul's argument in Romans 1:18–3:20?
    a. "For God shows no partiality" (Rom. 2:11).
    b. "We know that the judgment of God rightly falls on those who practice such things" (2:2).
    c. "God judges the secrets of men by Christ Jesus" (2:16).
    d. "None is righteous, no, not one" (3:10).
2. Which of the following is *not* perceived through general revelation or observations about human life apart from Scripture?
    a. The awareness of sin's reality
    b. The existence of God as Creator
    c. The good news of the gospel
    d. The religious impulse of man
3. What culture might be in view with the type of idolatry that Paul describes in Romans 1?
    a. Greeks
    b. Hebrews
    c. Egyptians
    d. Romans
4. Paul holds up homosexuality as the worst of all possible sins.
    a. True
    b. False
5. Paul's list of sins should make us pause and reflect on ourselves.
    a. True
    b. False
6. Who coined the phrase "passed away" in reference to people who have died?
    a. Mary Baker Eddy
    b. Charles Taze Russell
    c. Joseph Smith
    d. Ellen G. White

Answer Key—The Seriousness of Sin

REFLECTION & DISCUSSION QUESTIONS

Before the Video

What Do You Think?

These are personal questions. The answers should be based on your own knowledge and experience.

Scripture Reading

- What is God's response to idolatry?

  A sobering truth is that God hands us over to our sins when we suppress the truth about Him and become idolaters. In Romans 1:18, Paul says that this is a revelation of God's wrath, that even our sin is an expression of His judgment.

During the Video

Idolatry and Immorality

- What do we need to keep in mind when tracing Paul's arguments in Romans?

  Some of Paul's arguments can be complex, but to not get lost, we do well to keep in mind Paul's conclusions. Romans 1:18–3:20 forms a complete unit, and the conclusion to Paul's argument in this section is that there is none in all of humanity who are righteous. Keeping that in mind will help us see the structure of Paul's argument and Romans as a whole.

- What category within systematic theology is Paul employing in his argument in Romans 1? Define this category.

  Systematic theologians use the categories of general and special revelation to distinguish between the ways that God makes Himself known. Paul is basing his argument on the category of general revelation, which is the revelation of God's existence, power, and divine nature that is given universally to everyone through the natural created order.

- What do we see Paul modeling his argument that idolatry leads to immorality on?

  Paul first focuses on idolatry and then connects it to immorality. One has to deal with our relationship with God, and the other deals especially with our relationship with other people. Paul's argument follows the two tables of the moral law as summarized in the Ten Commandments. The first four commandments deal with our proper relation to God, and the second six commandments deal with our proper relation to other people.

"Little" Sins

- What misconception do we need to resist when considering Paul's list of sins in Romans 1?

  After hearing about the sins of idol worship and homosexuality as prime examples of debased minds that have turned from God, we may wonder why Paul lists what might seem to be minor sins in comparison. We must resist attempting to categorize greater and lesser sins, as though lesser sins were less offensive to God. Because God is holy, He is angry with all sin, and He cannot tolerate it in His presence.

- What might be Paul's intention for us in listing all these sins?

  While making sure that we understand that God condemns all manner of sin, Paul may also be listing various sins to bring us to a moment of reflection and ask ourselves, "So how do I measure up against all this?" It's a helpful question to ask ourselves, especially considering that Paul's purpose in this section of Romans is to set up why salvation is needed so that we marvel at how it has been provided.

After the Video

- Is it unjust for God to judge people who have not heard the gospel? Why or why not?

  Many people believe that it would be unjust for God to condemn people who have not heard the gospel, as if people need to have the opportunity to accept or reject the gospel. Paul's argument in Romans 1 is helpful for correcting this type of thinking, for it teaches that all people have enough knowledge of God to be without excuse for their idolatry and sin. God is just to judge, and He will not judge people based on what they did not know, but He will not overlook sin.

- Why does Paul bring up homosexuality in Romans 1? How is the veracity of Paul's argument in Romans 1 proved by recent LGBTQ activism?

  Paul does not point to homosexuality as the worst possible sin or expression of immorality, but he does highlight it because of how obviously it overturns God's order in creation. Homosexuality is a denial of God's creation of human beings as male and female. It violates the fundamental male-female distinction. Recent activism has moved beyond demanding that homosexuality and many other sins be accepted to demanding that they be celebrated, and many in our culture do just that (see Rom. 1:32).

- How is the reality of death handled in your family? Is it treated as a natural part of life or referred to in "polite" terms? How might Romans 1 equip you to talk about these things with your family?

  These questions are personal, but answers should reflect on the way that Paul underscores the seriousness of sin in Romans 1 by pointing to its penalty: death. Death is not a natural part of this life, but it is a testimony that sin is so serious that God punishes it through this awful reality. Paul does not shrink from the reality of death in Romans 1; he capitalizes on its reality as one of the reasons that we so desperately need the gospel.

REVIEW QUIZ

1. **D.**
Many of these passages deal with the seriousness of sin, especially as it relates to God's judgment of sin. Furthermore, all these deal with the universal scope of sin, which is at the heart of Paul's argument. We must remember that Paul is always working toward the conclusion that no one is righteous so that we don't misinterpret difficult passages in Romans 2 (see 3:10).

2. **C.**
Our natural observations of people throughout history teach us that we have an impulse to worship, and we are also painfully aware of sin both personally and societally. In some ways, the two go hand in hand. People worship the wrong things in their sin, suppressing the knowledge of God that they have through general revelation. What people do not have through general revelation, however, is knowledge of the good news of the gospel.

3. **C.**
Egyptian religion puzzled the ancients, especially the Romans and the Greeks, who did not understand the worship practices of the Egyptians, particularly in making idols of snakes or crocodiles. Although Paul has the idolatry of all the nations in view, idolatry as practiced in Egypt may be in Paul's mind as a prime example of idolatry among the nations.

4. **B.**
Dr. Godfrey stressed how God has made human beings as male and female, and sexual relationships are within the context of the marriage of one man and one woman. Therefore, homosexuality is a very obvious sin to hold up as an example of how people suppress the truth in unrighteousness, but it is not meant to be seen as the worst possible sin.

5. **A.**
Some of the sins that Paul lists in Romans 1 may be dismissed by some as "small sins," especially in comparison with others. But while God does not consider all sins equal, He will not tolerate any sin in His presence. In this sense, there are no "small sins." It may be tempting to read quickly through lists such as the one found in Romans 1, but we should slow down and evaluate ourselves against them, reminding ourselves of our need of the gospel.

6. **A.**
The reality of death bears witness to the seriousness of sin, but people have grown accustomed to not speaking about death in direct terms even when someone has

died. We might be more comfortable saying that someone "passed away" before saying that someone "died." The phrase "passed away" was coined by Mary Baker Eddy, who founded the Christian Science sect, which denies realities such as death and pain.

5

The Universality of Sin

INTRODUCTION

Not only is sin so serious that its penalty is death, but it is also universal in scope, "for all have sinned and fall short of the glory of God" (Rom. 3:23). In Romans 1, Paul condemned the idolatry and immorality of the nations, and in Romans 2, he charges the Israelites with not keeping the law. Dr. Godfrey traces Paul's argument to show how both gentiles *and* Jews are without excuse because what they know and what they do condemn them before a holy God.

LEARNING GOALS

When you have finished this lesson, you should be able to:

- Recognize the dangers of hypocrisy
- Describe how Paul stresses the first use of the law in Romans 2

KEY IDEAS

- We must first recognize our sin if we are to repent of it.
- Though the nations had not received special revelation as the Israelites had, they would still be judged on the basis of their innate understanding of the moral law.
- The law is not an external checklist but rather reveals something about us internally—the state of our hearts.

REFLECTION & DISCUSSION QUESTIONS

Before the Video

What Do You Think?

Take a moment to answer the following questions. They will prepare you for the lecture.

- Why are people more judgmental of others than they are of themselves?

- How did you know that something was wrong or a sin before you were a Christian?

Scripture Reading

> *In the meantime, when so many thousands of the people had gathered together that they were trampling one another, he began to say to his disciples first, "Beware of the leaven of the Pharisees, which is hypocrisy. Nothing is covered up that will not be revealed, or hidden that will not be known. Therefore whatever you have said in the dark shall be heard in the light, and what you have whispered in private rooms shall be proclaimed on the housetops."*
>
> —Luke 12:1–3

- What sobering reality about hypocrisy does Jesus teach here?

During the Video

Answer the following questions while you watch the video. They will guide you through the lecture.

The Judgment of Man and the Judgment of God — *0:00–11:00*

- What important shift does Paul make at the beginning of Romans 2? What is Paul attempting to expose?
- What do people commonly presume about God and His willingness to judge? How does Paul correct this presumption?
- What is a misinterpretation of God's rendering "to each one according to his works" (Rom. 2:6)?

The Law in Every Heart — *11:00–24:48*

- What remains in every human heart despite the fall?
- What was the boasting of the Jews over the gentiles?

- What is the first purpose of the law?

After the Video

Answer the following questions after you have finished the lecture. They will help you identify and summarize the major points.

- What did Dr. Godfrey call a besetting sin of moral people? How does Paul deal with this sin?

  If you are in a group, have the members consider some appropriate responses when we see the sins of others. Ask: When you see sin in someone's life, how should you approach him or her about it or reflect on yourself in light of it?

- In Romans, how does Paul set up a hypothetical way to be saved?

  If you are in a group, have the members talk about how God's righteous requirements in the law are foundational for our evangelism. Ask: How can you go about winsomely showing people that they fall short of even their own ethical standards, let alone God's perfect standard?

- Why does Paul bring up circumcision in his argument about the universality of sin?

  If you are in a group, have the members discuss ways in which they can reflect on their baptisms rightly and not presume on them in the manner that parallels first-century Jewish presumption on circumcision.

PRAYER

Commit what you have learned from God's Word in this lesson to prayer.

- Praise God for His righteousness as perfect Judge.
- Confess ways that you have condemned others of sin while excusing yourself.
- Thank God that He gives His people new hearts that yearn for more than outward conformity to His law.
- Ask God to use the law to drive you more deeply into Christ even as you strive to put sin to death and live more and more unto righteousness.

REVIEW QUIZ

Use these multiple-choice questions to measure what you learned from this lesson.

1. In the language of Romans 2:4, what do people presume on in their sin?
   a. God's judgment
   b. God's kindness
   c. God's grace
   d. God's wrath
2. Paul teaches that salvation is *theoretically* possible through our works in Romans 2.
   a. True
   b. False
3. What is *not* one of the three things that the one who receives eternal life perfectly strives for in Romans 2:7?
   a. Faith
   b. Glory
   c. Honor
   d. Immortality
4. Paul taught that Jews and Greeks would both be judged by the law in all its fullness as set forth in special revelation.
   a. True
   b. False
5. Which of the following is *not* one of the boasts that Paul ascribes to the Jews?
   a. Guides to the blind
   b. Instructors to the foolish
   c. Judges of unrighteousness
   d. Lights to those in darkness
6. What is the great or first purpose of the law?
   a. To promote worship
   b. To foster holy living
   c. To restrain evil
   d. To expose sin

Answer Key—The Universality of Sin

REFLECTION & DISCUSSION QUESTIONS

Before the Video

What Do You Think?

These are personal questions. The answers should be based on your own knowledge and experience.

Scripture Reading

- What sobering reality about hypocrisy does Jesus teach here?

  The Pharisees exhibited an outward righteousness, the substance of which they did not possess at the level of their hearts. As hypocrites, they professed to be what they did not intend to be. In this passage, Jesus teaches us about the sobering reality that hypocrisy will one day be exposed in the light of God's judgment. Even if an inward unrighteousness escapes the notice of others, it does not escape the notice of God.

During the Video

The Judgment of Man and the Judgment of God

- What important shift does Paul make at the beginning of Romans 2? What is Paul attempting to expose?

  Paul shifts focus from thinking about sin in the context of the nations in Romans 1 to questioning the sin that exists among God's people. This shift can be seen in Paul's redirection of his comments in the phrase "O man." In doing this, Paul is trying to expose hypocrisy and self-righteousness. Just as those who suppress the truth in unrighteousness are without excuse, so are those who judge sin and yet commit it.

- What do people commonly presume about God and His willingness to judge? How does Paul correct this presumption?

  People often dismiss the idea that God is angry, thinking that because He has yet to judge sin, then He must not be angry about it. Paul corrects this presumption by pointing out that the patience of God that causes people to doubt God's anger against sin is not a sign of His excusing our sin but a sign of His patience that we might repent of our sin.

- What is a misinterpretation of God's rendering "to each one according to his works" (Rom. 2:6)?

  One misinterpretation is to think that Paul has in mind a works-based righteousness that is achievable before God, that God will "give eternal life" (2:7) even to those who are not perfectly righteous, as if our good could outweigh our bad.

The Law in Every Heart

- What remains in every human heart despite the fall?

  Paul says, "For when Gentiles, who do not have the law, by nature do what the law requires, they are a law to themselves, even though they do not have the law" (Rom. 2:14). There is a law in every human heart that is the remnants of the moral law that testifies to people when they do right and wrong. On the basis of this law, even those without special revelation will still be condemned by the law.

- What was the boasting of the Jews over the gentiles?

  The Jews boasted in their reception of the law and their relationship with God, seeing themselves, to use the language of the Apostle Paul, as guides to the blind, lights to those who are in darkness, instructors of the foolish, and teachers of children (Rom. 2:19–20). Paul challenges this boast with the question, "You then who teach others, do you not teach yourself?" (v. 21).

- What is the first purpose of the law?

  The first or great purpose of the law is to help us recognize that we are sinners. This is the Apostle Paul's teaching both for gentiles, who had only the remnants of the moral law on their hearts, and for Jews, who had the fullness of God's law as revealed in Scripture.

After the Video

- What did Dr. Godfrey call a besetting sin of moral people? How does Paul deal with this sin?

  Human beings throughout history have set themselves up as judges, condemning others while excusing themselves. Dr. Godfrey called this sin of self-righteousness and hypocrisy "one of the great besetting sins of moral people." Paul deals with this sin by driving home the inconsistency in judging others while still committing the very sins that we judge. By exposing self-righteousness and hypocrisy, Paul underscores that even those who seem moral are without excuse before God.

- In Romans, how does Paul set up a hypothetical way to be saved?

  In Romans 2:6–7, Paul writes that God "will render to each one according to his works: to those who by patience in well-doing seek for glory and honor and immortality, he will give eternal life." In stating this, Paul presents his understanding of how someone is justified by works, but this does not mean that Paul believes that works are a possible means by which we can be declared righteous, for obedience to God's law must be perfect. In this sense, we cannot be justified by works; we must be justified through the works of another—Jesus Christ.

- Why does Paul bring up circumcision in his argument about the universality of sin?

  Paul discusses outward and inward circumcision in Romans 2:25–29 to teach that outward conformity to the law of God is not enough. Even the sign of circumcision was intended to point toward an inward reality. It was not a merely physical sign; it was supposed to represent something spiritual. Circumcision was a sign of the covenant of grace and was never intended to be rested in as if it were a sign of one's righteousness by works.

REVIEW QUIZ

1. **C.**
   Paul does not use the word grace *to describe the presumption that people have when they feel at ease in their judgments of others and yet sin themselves. Paul does use the word "kindness," however, along with "forbearance" and "patience," in Romans 2:4, which better describe God's disposition toward sinners in giving them time to repent.*

2. **A.**
   It would be problematic to affirm that our works can actually secure our salvation, but Paul does not believe this is possible because his entire argument that spans the first three chapters of Romans is leading to the conclusion that all of us have fallen short of God's glory in our sin (Rom. 3:23). Paul does, however, present this as a theoretical possibility so that his readers might grapple with the righteous expectations of God for perfect obedience.

3. **A.**
   In Romans 2:6–7, Paul writes, "He will render to each one according to his works: to those who by patience in well-doing seek for glory and honor and immortality, he will give eternal life." The challenging thing is that no one perfectly lives in pursuit of those realities.

4. **B.**
   Whereas Paul teaches that both Jews and Greeks will be judged, he does not teach that God will judge people for what they do not know. Romans 2:12–16 bears witness to the reality that the gentiles did not have the law but that the remnants of the moral law of God remain on their hearts as part of God's general revelation.

5. **C.**
   Paul sees the judgment of the Jews as something to be credited to their shame. All these other descriptions, however, were the great intended privileges for the Jews as those who had received God's Word, and we ought to desire to be guides to the blind, lights to those in darkness, and instructors of the foolish ourselves in accordance with righteousness.

6. **D.**
Dr. Godfrey defined what he called the great or first purpose of the law as its ability to wake us up to the reality that we are sinners. This accords with the threefold use of the law in historic Reformed thought. The first use of the law reveals to us our sin. The second use of the law is to restrain evil. The third use of the law is to guide us to good works in the Christian life.

6

The Righteousness through Faith

INTRODUCTION

After discussing the seriousness of sin and the universal scope of sin, Paul is ready to transition to sin's remedy—not a righteousness through the law but a righteousness by faith in Jesus Christ. Using one verse from the Old Testament after the other, Paul shows us our need. In this lesson, Dr. Godfrey illumines how Paul teaches that the Old Testament and the New Testament are in agreement about the only way to be saved.

LEARNING GOALS

When you have finished this lesson, you should be able to:

- Understand Paul's intent in his many quotations from the Old Testament as well as some of their implications for how we read Scripture and relate to others
- Defend the consistency between the teaching of salvation in the Old and New Testaments
- Explain Paul's great transitional statements away from the condemnation of the law to the person and work of Christ

KEY IDEAS

- Paul's use of the Old Testament in Romans demonstrates that the message of salvation in the Old Testament and in the New Testament is the same.
- The battle between Christianity and Judaism is one between two different religions, and this fact should measure how we understand sharp statements against the Jews in Scripture.
- Jesus has done for us what we could not have done for ourselves, so righteousness is not achieved through our own law-keeping but through faith in Another who has perfectly kept the law.

REFLECTION & DISCUSSION QUESTIONS

Before the Video

What Do You Think?

Take a moment to answer the following questions. They will prepare you for the lecture.

- What has been the most challenging thing to study or reflect on so far in Romans?
- How can it be that God both hates sin and is able to forgive sinners?

Scripture Reading

Do not remember against us our former iniquities; let your compassion come speedily to meet us, for we are brought very low. Help us, O God of our salvation, for the glory of your name; deliver us, and atone for our sins, for your name's sake!

—Psalm 79:8–9

- How is the concept that we are not saved by virtue of our works taught in this passage from the Old Testament?

During the Video

Answer the following questions while you watch the video. They will guide you through the lecture.

Paul's Use of the Old Testament *0:00–14:50*

- Why is it significant that Paul quotes from Psalm 51?
- How does Paul's allusion to Psalm 143:2 help us to see how the Old Testament pointed forward to Christ?
- How do the Apostolic reading of the Old Testament and the rabbinic reading of the Old Testament differ?

The Great Transition *14:50–24:52*

- Summarize the transition from Romans 3:20 to 3:21.

- What are propitiation and expiation?

After the Video

Answer the following questions after you have finished the lecture. They will help you identify and summarize the major points.

- What needs to be reconciled about Paul's quotations from the Psalms, and how?

  If you are in a group, have the members discuss how they have had difficulty interpreting the Old Testament in the past. Ask: Why would it make sense that the message of the Old and New Testaments is the same? How might this consistency encourage you when facing difficulties in interpreting the Old Testament?

- How does the antagonism between differing readings of the Old Testament emerge in the Gospels?

  If you are in a group, have the members read Mark 2:23–28 and discuss how the principle of unity between the Old and New Testaments might speak to how we observe the Lord's Day. Ask: What must we be careful about to not become like the Pharisees?

- Romans 3:26 reads concerning the propitiation accomplished through the blood of Christ, "It was to show his righteousness at the present time, so that he might be just and the justifier of the one who has faith in Jesus." What does this mean?

  If you are in a group, have the members discuss how such a passage makes them feel about their sin *and* their salvation.

PRAYER

Commit what you have learned from God's Word in this lesson to prayer.

- Praise God for being just and the justifier for those in Christ.
- Confess ways that you fail to acknowledge the sinfulness of your sin.
- Thank God that as He makes you more aware of your sin, He also gives you a great appreciation for His grace.
- Ask God to use your experience of His grace to give you a deeper concern for the lost.

REVIEW QUIZ

Use these multiple-choice questions to measure what you learned from this lesson.

1. Paul quotes from which psalm in Romans 3:4 when he writes, "That you may be justified in your words, and prevail when you are judged"?
   a. Psalm 26
   b. Psalm 51
   c. Psalm 90
   d. Psalm 143

2. What other book of the Bible does Paul quote from in Romans 3:10–18 besides the Psalms?
   a. Deuteronomy
   b. Exodus
   c. Isaiah
   d. Leviticus

3. The Old Testament upholds the possibility of moral perfection.
   a. True
   b. False

4. The transition from Romans 3:20 to 3:21 enters us into what section of Romans?
   a. "Salvation Needed"
   b. "Salvation Provided"
   c. "Salvation Experienced"
   d. "Salvation Lived Out"

5. Expiation is the turning away of God's wrath.
   a. True
   b. False

6. What word shares the same root in Greek as *righteousness*?
   a. Justification
   b. Propitiation
   c. Purification
   d. Sanctification

Answer Key—The Righteousness through Faith

REFLECTION & DISCUSSION QUESTIONS

Before the Video

What Do You Think?

These are personal questions. The answers should be based on your own knowledge and experience.

Scripture Reading

- How is the concept that we are not saved by virtue of our works taught in this passage from the Old Testament?

  In Psalm 79, the psalmist clearly acknowledges his sin along with the sin of the nation of Israel. There is an admission of a real lack of righteousness that needs to be atoned for, and the psalmist bases his appeal for redemption not on any deeds done but on the mercy and grace of God. Such redemption is for His "name's sake"—for His glory alone.

During the Video

Paul's Use of the Old Testament

- Why is it significant that Paul quotes from Psalm 51?

  Psalm 51 is the great psalm of contrition from King David. David was one of the most holy leaders in Israel, but in Psalm 51, he confesses his sin. When David confesses himself to be a sinner before God, he also upholds God's blamelessness in judging every sinner.

- How does Paul's allusion to Psalm 143:2 help us to see how the Old Testament pointed forward to Christ?

  Paul alludes to Psalm 143:2 in Romans 3:20 when he says, "For by works of the law no human being will be justified in his sight, since through the law comes knowledge of sin." Psalm 143:2 states that no one is righteous before God, which shows how the Old Testament bears witness to our spiritual need, pointing us forward to Jesus Christ as its solution. By declaring everyone unrighteous, the Old Testament pointed to our need of a Savior.

- How do the Apostolic reading of the Old Testament and the rabbinic reading of the Old Testament differ?

  The Apostolic reading of the Old Testament is precisely what we see in Paul's many quotations of the Psalms, that everyone is a sinner who needs to be saved by the mercy of God. But the rabbinic reading of the Old Testament, which was popular in Jesus' day as well as Paul's and ever since, is that one is saved by keeping the law.

The Great Transition

- Summarize the transition from Romans 3:20 to 3:21.

  In Romans 3:20, Paul sets forth a major problem for every sinner: "By works of the law no human being will be justified in his sight." How, then, can we be justified? This is Paul's major transition to gospel; Romans 3:21 begins with the word "now." A great shift has taken place, and now God's righteousness is found through faith in Jesus Christ, who bore God's righteous judgment on behalf of His people.

- What are propitiation and expiation?

  In Romans 3:25, we are told that God put forward His Son, Jesus Christ, "as a propitiation." Christ's blood both covers our sin and averts God's wrath. The covering of our sin is called expiation. *The averting or satisfying of God's wrath is called* propitiation. *For all who believe, both these realities occurred at the cross when God judged sin in Christ, which is how God is able to be just and yet pardon sinners.*

After the Video

- What needs to be reconciled about Paul's quotations from the Psalms, and how?

  Paul quotes from numerous psalms that condemn the wicked, but these psalms also commend the righteous. On the surface, this may seem like a problem because Paul's argument is leading to the conclusion that all *have fallen short of the glory of God. How, then, can some be righteous? These psalms, however, do not imagine people who are righteous in their own right, but point to those who recognize their sin and trust in the Lord. The righteous in the Psalms are not those who are sinless but those who are saved, not through works of the law but through God's mercy and trusting in His promises.*

- How does the antagonism between differing readings of the Old Testament emerge in the Gospels?

  This antagonism is primarily revealed through the exchanges between Jesus and the Pharisees. The Pharisees are the origin of the rabbinic reading of the Old Testament that asserts a possibility of achieving righteousness through the law. Jesus constantly confronted the Pharisees on account of their hypocrisy and their ignorance. His confrontation with the Pharisees about the Sabbath is one example of this. The gospel writers exposed the weakness of the Pharisees' interpretation of the Old Testament by recording how Jesus left them silent and unable to answer His questions even about the law that they claimed to be experts in.

- Romans 3:26 reads concerning the propitiation accomplished through the blood of Christ, "It was to show his righteousness at the present time, so that he might be just and the justifier of the one who has faith in Jesus." What does this mean?

  In His divine forbearance, God formerly passed over sin before the time of Jesus Christ, but He fully judged sin at His Son's death on the cross. In this judgment, God demonstrated His righteousness, that He would not allow sin to go unpunished. God is just. At the same time, God is also able to be the justifier of those who believe because Jesus Christ has borne the penalty of their sin.

REVIEW QUIZ

1. **B.**
   Though these are not some of the most famous words in David's great psalm of repentance, they are from Psalm 51, which Paul quotes in Romans 3:4 to underscore God's righteousness in judgment.

2. **C.**
   In Romans 3:10–18, Paul quotes numerous verses of the Old Testament, primarily from the Psalms, to bolster his position that no one is righteous before God. Though Paul argues that the Law and the Prophets both support his teaching on justification, he quotes only from Isaiah in this string of quotations.

3. **B.**
   While the Old Testament calls us to moral perfection, it does not imply that our attainment of moral perfection is possible. Those who are called "righteous" and "blameless" in Scripture are those who live by faith in God's covenant promises.

4. **B.**
   Romans 3:21 introduces the third section of Dr. Godfrey's outline, "Salvation Provided." After setting up the seriousness of sin and its universal scope, Paul is now ready to offer up the hope of the gospel as the answer to our predicament.

5. **B.**
   Propitiation is the turning away of God's wrath. In propitiation, God's wrath is assuaged or satisfied. In expiation, our sins are covered. Psalm 103:12 is a good description of our relationship to our sins once they have been expiated in Christ: "As far as the east is from the west, so far does he remove our transgressions from us."

6. **A.**
   The Greek term rendered "justified" in English in Romans 3:24 shares the same Greek root as the word righteousness. *When Paul introduces the idea of justification in this verse, it is directly connected to the righteousness that God manifests and provides in Christ.*

7

The Law of Works & the Law of Faith

INTRODUCTION

In the opening chapters of Romans, Paul has helped us understand why salvation is needed, and now he develops how God has made salvation possible apart from the law through faith in Jesus Christ. In this lesson, Dr. Godfrey continues Paul's argument for justification by faith from Romans 3:21–4:12, showing how Paul's message is consistent with how God has always operated with His people.

LEARNING GOALS

When you have finished this lesson, you should be able to:

- Understand the nature of faith
- Explain how justification by faith is connected to the relationship between Israel and the nations
- Summarize Paul's defense of justification by faith through the lives of Abraham and David

KEY IDEAS

- The nature of faith can be distorted such that people think of faith as a work through which we earn our forgiveness, but faith is the instrument of our justification and not the grounds for it.
- God's covenant with Abraham, the father of faith, reveals that the covenant of grace is based not on works but on faith.
- The great blessing that David longed for was not to secure his standing before God through his own righteousness but to have his sins mercifully covered.

REFLECTION & DISCUSSION QUESTIONS

Before the Video

What Do You Think?

Take a moment to answer the following questions. They will prepare you for the lecture.

- Does faith earn us anything with God? Why or why not?
- Why would Paul use the examples of Abraham and David to bolster his case for justification by faith?

Scripture Reading

After these things the word of the LORD came to Abram in a vision: "Fear not, Abram, I am your shield; your reward shall be very great." But Abram said, "O Lord GOD, what will you give me, for I continue childless, and the heir of my house is Eliezer of Damascus?" And Abram said, "Behold, you have given me no offspring, and a member of my household will be my heir." And behold, the word of the LORD came to him: "This man shall not be your heir; your very own son shall be your heir." And he brought him outside and said, "Look toward heaven, and number the stars, if you are able to number them." Then he said to him, "So shall your offspring be." And he believed the LORD, and he counted it to him as righteousness.

—Genesis 15:1–6

- Why is Abraham counted righteous? Why is this significant for Paul's purposes in Romans?

During the Video

Answer the following questions while you watch the video. They will guide you through the lecture.

The Nature of Faith — *0:00–10:58*

- Why does Paul use the phrase "law of faith" (Rom. 3:27) if he is not setting up another type of work?
- What is the essential character of faith?

- What is Paul's primary point in briefly introducing the idea of justification by faith in Romans 3?

The Faith of Abraham and David *10:58–24:35*

- What could be anticipated in God's promise to Abraham? What designation is then given to Abraham for how he responded to God's promise?

- Why did David especially hope for the blessedness of one whose sins are covered?

After the Video

Answer the following questions after you have finished the lecture. They will help you identify and summarize the major points.

- Paul says, "For we hold that one is justified by faith apart from works of the law" (Rom. 3:28). How have some misinterpreted the phrase "works of the law"? How does John Calvin interpret this phrase?

  If you are in a group, have the members discuss why one's understanding about the nature of faith directly connects to the gospel. Ask: Have you ever thought of your faith as a type of work? How do we free ourselves of this type of thinking?

- How was Abraham misunderstood by the rabbis of Paul's day? How does Paul correct this in his letter to the Romans?

  If you are in a group, have the members read James 2:14–24. Ask: How do you reconcile Paul's teaching about faith, works, and Abraham with this passage?

- How did Thomas Aquinas think about justification? How is that view out of accord with Paul's teaching in Romans?

  If you are in a group, have the members discuss how our sanctification relates to our justification in such a way that our growth in grace doesn't contribute to our justification. Ask: Why does our sanctification even matter?

PRAYER

Commit what you have learned from God's Word in this lesson to prayer.

- Praise God for His sovereign power as demonstrated throughout history.
- Confess any tendency you have to boast in yourself, losing sight of Christ's finished work.
- Thank God for the examples of faith that we have in Old Testament saints, such as Abraham and David, who did not cling to their own righteousness.
- Ask God to help you to see the beauty of the Christian life of obedience that is rooted in faith.

REVIEW QUIZ

Use these multiple-choice questions to measure what you learned from this lesson.

1. Why does Paul use the phrase "law of faith" in Romans 3:27?
    a. To add a new requirement
    b. To equate the law with faith
    c. For a sense of literary balance
    d. For theological precision
2. An essential characteristic of faith is that it looks inward.
    a. True
    b. False
3. Which of the following is in the correct order?
    a. Abraham's call, Abraham's circumcision, Abraham's justification
    b. Abraham's justification, Abraham's call, Abraham's circumcision
    c. Abraham's circumcision, Abraham's justification, Abraham's call
    d. Abraham's call, Abraham's justification, Abraham's circumcision
4. One teaching of Thomas Aquinas does injustice to which of the following phrases?
    a. "Through the law comes knowledge of sin" (Rom. 3:20)
    b. "All have sinned and fall short of the glory of God" (3:23)
    c. "Wages are not counted as a gift but as his due" (4:4)
    d. "Believes in him who justifies the ungodly" (4:5)
5. John Calvin believed that Paul was referring to the performance of God's law when he said, "One is justified by faith apart from works of the law" (Rom. 3:28).
    a. True
    b. False

6. Which of the following did Dr. Godfrey connect to the work of Jesus Christ?
    a. Understanding the nature of grace
    b. Understanding Jew-gentile relations
    c. Understanding the nature of the law
    d. All of the above

Answer Key—The Law of Works & the Law of Faith

REFLECTION & DISCUSSION QUESTIONS

Before the Video

What Do You Think?

These are personal questions. The answers should be based on your own knowledge and experience.

Scripture Reading

- Why is Abraham counted righteous? Why is this significant for Paul's purposes in Romans?

  Throughout Romans, Paul is correcting a misinterpretation of the Old Testament that perpetuated the belief that righteousness is attained through the law. This episode in Abraham's life, in which he is counted righteous because he believed God, supports Paul's argument for justification by faith, something that is explicitly taught in the Old Testament and with no one short of Abraham.

During the Video

The Nature of Faith

- Why does Paul use the phrase "law of faith" (Rom. 3:27) if he is not setting up another type of work?

  Paul uses the phrase "law of faith" in Romans 3:27 as a literary parallel that balances the phrase "law of works." Paul is not setting up a new requirement through which we earn our salvation. Though he used the phrase "obedience of faith" earlier in Romans 1, these phrases are not intended to communicate the idea that faith is just another work that we perform to secure our salvation on our own.

- What is the essential character of faith?

  The essential character of faith is that it looks away from itself. Having faith does not mean that we look to the quality of our faith for assurance. Rather, we look not to ourselves but to Christ. Exercising faith is indeed something that we do, but faith itself is not what saves us.

- What is Paul's primary point in briefly introducing the idea of justification by faith in Romans 3?

  Paul's introduction of justification by faith is set within a larger argument dealing with the relationship between Jews and gentiles. After teaching that all have fallen short of God's glory through sin and are justified only apart from works of the law (Rom. 3:21–28), Paul immediately begins to talk about Jews and gentiles (vv. 29–30), who all have a share in God's way of salvation through faith.

The Faith of Abraham and David

- What could be anticipated in God's promise to Abraham? What designation is then given to Abraham for how he responded to God's promise?

  In Genesis 12, God promised Abraham that all the families of the earth would be blessed through him. Jesus Christ is, of course, in view in this promise, but we can also anticipate how God would one day bring the gentiles into the people of God. Because Abraham believed God, he can therefore be called the "father of faith." Paul calls him "the father of all who believe without being circumcised" (Rom. 4:11).

- Why did David especially hope for the blessedness of one whose sins are covered?

  In Psalm 32, David said, "Blessed is the one whose transgression is forgiven, whose sin is covered" (v. 1). David especially needed a covering for sin because of the grievous sins he committed surrounding Bathsheba. Such great sins as adultery and murder did not have specific sacrifices, but God could remain righteous and forgive David's sin by sending His Son as a substitute for David and all others who believe.

After the Video

- Paul says, "For we hold that one is justified by faith apart from works of the law" (Rom. 3:28). How have some misinterpreted the phrase "works of the law"? How does John Calvin interpret this phrase?

  In the history of the church, there has been a debate about the meaning of the phrase "works of the law." Some have believed Paul to be referring to some kind of lesser work or a type of work that is fueled by selfish egoism. Calvin, on the other hand, affirms that Paul is referring to the law in an ordinary biblical sense. The works of the law that Paul has in mind are the best types of works because the law reveals to us what is pleasing to God, though we cannot keep these perfectly for our justification.

- How was Abraham misunderstood by the rabbis of Paul's day? How does Paul correct this in his letter to the Romans?

  The rabbinical tradition held that Abraham was justified by works, that he led a holy life, and that he is therefore a model for holiness. Paul understood this, however, to be a radical misinterpretation of the most pivotal figure of the Old Testament. To remedy this, Paul takes the Romans all the way back to Genesis 15, before Abraham was even circumcised, to show that he was justified by faith before doing any work that could be seen to be consistent with the law.

- How did Thomas Aquinas think about justification? How is that view out of accord with Paul's teaching in Romans?

  Romans 4:5 teaches us that God is the One "who justifies the ungodly." This phrase has challenged various Christian traditions through the ages. Thomas Aquinas, for instance, understood justification in such a way that God can declare us righteous because we actually are righteous. In other words, God makes us righteous in the Christian life and so can declare us to be justified in His sight. Paul does not teach, however, that we can somehow add something to Christ's work, as though our righteousness contributed to our justification. This is the literal sense of what it means that God "justifies the ungodly" and not that He justifies because the ungodly have become godly, though this progression is true of the Christian life.

REVIEW QUIZ

1. **C.**
   While Paul, a brilliant theological mind, cannot by any means be called imprecise, he likely used the phrase "law of faith" in Romans 3:27 to balance that phrase with which it stands in juxtaposition: "law of works."

2. **B.**
   Faith is not the object of faith. We do not look to our faith for our justification. Rather, we look away from ourselves and to Jesus Christ when we exercise saving faith in Him.

3. **D.**
   It is critical to remember that Abraham was counted righteous by his faith and not by any work that he had done. He was counted righteous before he was circumcised. A simple but important lesson in justification is that Genesis 15 comes before Genesis 17.

4. **D.**
   The teaching of Thomas Aquinas that Dr. Godfrey raised to our awareness in this lesson relates most to the wonderful phrase from Romans 4:5 that God "justifies the ungodly." Thomas taught that God is able to justify sinners because He makes them justifiable. In other words, He makes them righteous. But Paul teaches that God justifies the ungodly.

5. **A.**
   Although some have interpreted the phrase "works of the law" as something other than God's law as revealed in Scripture, Calvin did not. He believed with Paul that someone can be justified fully before God through faith without anything in addition to that faith.

6. **D.**
   While it may not immediately seem that the relationship between Jews and gentiles directly relates to the work of Christ, Paul connects the two intentionally in

Romans. Just as Christ's work helps us understand this issue, it teaches us about the nature of grace, the law, and the whole of the Christian life.

8

Abraham: The Father of the Faithful

INTRODUCTION

Abraham can be considered the father of all who believe because he had faith even before he was circumcised. Mere national markers do not make someone a part of Abraham's family. Paul helps us see that truth in Romans as he deals with the nature of the law and justification by faith. In this lesson, Dr. Godfrey explains how the law has been fulfilled in Christ and why we ought to model our faith after the faith of Abraham.

LEARNING GOALS

When you have finished this lesson, you should be able to:

- Explain why Paul can condemn circumcision in one place of the Bible and yet seemingly approve of it in another
- Define what the sacraments are as signs and seals
- Articulate a biblical definition of hope and faith

KEY IDEAS

- The promise that was made to Abraham was fulfilled in the coming of Jesus Christ.
- Paul understood that Abraham possessed a strong faith, that despite everything that could cause him to doubt, he trusted in the promises of God.
- Our experiences are not always easy, but always ought to be underwritten by a faith that looks to the God who brings life from the dead and existence out of nonexistence.

REFLECTION & DISCUSSION QUESTIONS

Before the Video

What Do You Think?

Take a moment to answer the following questions. They will prepare you for the lecture.

- What astounds you about Abraham's faith? What might make you question its strength?
- What does it mean to be hopeful about the future? How is hope connected to faith?

Scripture Reading

And God said to Abraham, "As for you, you shall keep my covenant, you and your offspring after you throughout their generations. This is my covenant, which you shall keep, between me and you and your offspring after you: Every male among you shall be circumcised. You shall be circumcised in the flesh of your foreskins, and it shall be a sign of the covenant between me and you. He who is eight days old among you shall be circumcised. Every male throughout your generations, whether born in your house or bought with your money from any foreigner who is not of your offspring, both he who is born in your house and he who is bought with your money, shall surely be circumcised. So shall my covenant be in your flesh an everlasting covenant. Any uncircumcised male who is not circumcised in the flesh of his foreskin shall be cut off from his people; he has broken my covenant."

—Genesis 17:9–14

- Why might adherence to circumcision have been a point of conflict in Paul's day in light of this passage?

During the Video

Answer the following questions while you watch the video. They will guide you through the lecture.

Promise Fulfilled *0:00–6:52*

- How is Paul able to condemn adherence to circumcision in Galatians 5, yet have Timothy circumcised in Acts 16?

- What was circumcision originally a sign of? How was it fulfilled?

Hope and Faith *6:52–18:40*

- What events are evoked by the phrase about our God "who gives life to the dead and calls into existence the things that do not exist" (Rom. 4:17)?

- What is hope? What is a difference between hope and faith?

Our Boast *18:40–24:48*

- What are the two ways that we ought to understand our peace with God?

- What, surprisingly, did Paul consider to be a source of our boasting?

After the Video

Answer the following questions after you have finished the lecture. They will help you identify and summarize the major points.

- Considering circumcision as a sign and seal, why would it be inconsistent to see it as necessary for one's justification? What are signs and seals, and what is the danger of this inconsistency?

  If you are in a group, have the members read Galatians 3:15–29 and discuss the various ways that Paul talks about the law. Ask: What lines of Paul's thought stick out to you?

- What is an important lesson to learn from Abraham about the nature of faith and our own faith?

  If you are in a group, have the members quickly skim through Genesis 12–25, finding places in the story of Abraham that make us question his faith and those that show us just how strong his faith was.

- How does Paul's thought in Romans 5 demonstrate that he is a "realist" when it comes to the Christian life? How have you experienced or processed difficult circumstances in the Christian life?

  If you are in a group, have the members identify and discuss when suffering in their lives turned out to be for their good in the Christian life.

PRAYER

Commit what you have learned from God's Word in this lesson to prayer.

- Praise God that He has provided access to His grace through faith in Jesus Christ.
- Confess times when you have doubted God's goodness or love for you in times of suffering.
- Thank God for the Holy Spirit, who has been given to us and enables us to experience His love.
- Ask God to help you bear suffering in the power of the Holy Spirit and in the knowledge that even it will increase your hope in the Christian life.

REVIEW QUIZ

Use these multiple-choice questions to measure what you learned from this lesson.

1. Paul allowed Timothy to be circumcised because circumcision is a matter of indifference.
   a. True
   b. False
2. In this lesson, which theologian did we learn offers a helpful corrective to understanding the nature of faith?
   a. John Brown
   b. John Bunyan
   c. John Calvin
   d. John Owen
3. What is an alternative translation for the Greek word that is translated "rejoice" in Romans 5:2 and 5:3?
   a. "Adore"
   b. "Boast"
   c. "Glorify"
   d. "Praise"

4. Which of the following was *not* mentioned by Dr. Godfrey in connection to the phrase about God "who gives life to the dead and calls into existence the things that do not exist" (Rom. 4:17)?
    a. Abraham's "lifeless" body
    b. Abraham's sacrifice of Isaac
    c. Christ's resurrection
    d. God's work of creation
5. Romans 4 is a strong reinforcement of the nature of Abraham's faith.
    a. True
    b. False
6. Which of the following is *not* an outcome of suffering, as recorded in Romans 5?
    a. Character
    b. Endurance
    c. Hope
    d. Love

Answer Key—Abraham: The Father of the Faithful

REFLECTION & DISCUSSION QUESTIONS

Before the Video

What Do You Think?

These are personal questions. The answers should be based on your own knowledge and experience.

Scripture Reading

- Why might adherence to circumcision have been a point of conflict in Paul's day in light of this passage?

  Circumcision was the sign and seal of God's covenant with Abraham. In this passage, strong language is used to communicate the enduring nature of this sign between God and His people. It is called an "everlasting covenant" that was to be kept by Abraham's offspring "throughout their generations" such that anyone who was not circumcised would be "cut off from his people."

During the Video

Promise Fulfilled

- How is Paul able to condemn adherence to circumcision in Galatians 5, yet have Timothy circumcised in Acts 16?

  Paul's strong remarks in Galatians that one who adheres to circumcision would be "severed from Christ" (Gal. 5:4) must be understood within the context of the legalism that threatened the churches of Galatia. It was being taught that the Mosaic law needed to be kept for someone to be saved, but Paul taught that circumcision was a matter of indifference in light of Christ (see 5:6; 6:15). This is why he could have Timothy circumcised in Acts 16; it was not adding anything to Timothy's justification before God.

- What was circumcision originally a sign of? How was it fulfilled?

  Circumcision originally was a sign and seal of the covenant of grace pointing to the promise of God that would be fulfilled in the offspring of Abraham. The substance and fulfillment of that promise was Jesus Christ, the true offspring of Abraham (see Gal. 3:16).

Hope and Faith

- What events are evoked by the phrase about our God "who gives life to the dead and calls into existence the things that do not exist" (Rom. 4:17)?

  Paul writes this phrase in reference to Abraham, so Abraham's circumstance and old age in light of God's promises of a child are certainly in view. This phrase is also evocative of the creation of the world ex nihilo, *out of nothing, and the resurrection of Jesus Christ from the dead, which includes our new life in Christ.*

- What is hope? What is a difference between hope and faith?

  Hope was defined as a confidence or assurance in what God has promised to do in the future. Dr. Godfrey distinguished hope from faith in a temporal sense, hope dealing with the future and faith dealing with the present.

Our Boast

- What are the two ways that we ought to understand our peace with God?

  Through the work of Christ, "we have peace with God" (Rom. 5:1). Paul's use of the word "peace" here can be understood in two ways: objectively and subjectively. Objectively, we have peace with God because there is no more animosity between us and God; He is satisfied with the finished work of His Son. Subjectively, we experience the sense of peace that we have in that relationship with God.

- What, surprisingly, did Paul consider to be a source of our boasting?

  Not only did Paul proclaim that we "boast" (translated "rejoice" in the ESV) in the hope of the glory of God (Rom. 5:2), but he also said that we "boast" (also translated "rejoice" in the ESV) in our sufferings (v. 3). Paul did not deny the hard realities of the Christian life.

After the Video

- Considering circumcision as a sign and seal, why would it be inconsistent to see it as necessary for one's justification? What are signs and seals, and what is the danger of this inconsistency?

  The sacraments as signs are visible indications of God's promise. As seals, they are God's guarantees of His promise. In the case of circumcision, it was administered as a sign of the covenant of grace that would be fulfilled in the offspring of Abraham, who is Jesus Christ. The One to whom circumcision pointed is the One in whom we are justified through faith. It would be inconsistent, therefore, to consider circumcision as something that contributes to our justification. If we were to think this way about circumcision as the Judaizers of Galatians did, or even about baptism as the corresponding sign of the new covenant, then we would be exposed to God's wrath in attempting to be justified by the law, "for the law brings wrath" (Rom. 4:15).

- What is an important lesson to learn from Abraham about the nature of faith and our own faith?

  Through Abraham's story, not only do we learn about faith as an instrument of justification, but we also learn about what true faith looks like. We may be surprised to hear Paul's description of Abraham's rich faith, especially when we look at some of the moments in his life that don't appear to be particularly faithful. Yet despite all his struggles, Abraham kept trusting the promises of God. This encourages us during our own moments of difficulty and doubt to keep trusting the Lord, and this trust is a testimony of the strength of our faith and not its weakness. In fact, as John Calvin said, our faith is our strength in times of weakness.

- How does Paul's thought in Romans 5 demonstrate that he is a "realist" when it comes to the Christian life? How have you experienced or processed difficult circumstances in the Christian life?

  The second question is personal, but Paul bears witness that suffering is part of the Christian life in Romans 5. He does not deny these realities even in light of the glorious access to God's grace and peace that we have through Christ. Furthermore, Paul rejoices that suffering bears good fruit in our lives: endurance, character, and hope (Rom. 5:4).

REVIEW QUIZ

1. **A.**
   Although Paul spoke adamantly against the Judaizers, who believed that circumcision was required for justification, he allowed Timothy to be circumcised. This is because they were neither adhering to the rite for justification nor acting out of concession to the Judaizers. In another instance, however, Paul would not allow Titus to be circumcised so as not to confirm the message of the Judaizers (Gal. 2:2–5).

2. **C.**
   We typically think of doubt as a sign that we have a weak faith, which calls us to question our source of strength in the Christian life. In book 3 of the Institutes of the Christian Religion, *John Calvin wrote about faith in such a way that we can rightly see faith as our bulwark and shield through struggles and doubts and not something that can be characterized by weakness.*

3. **B.**
   Elsewhere in Romans, the ESV translates the same Greek word that is used in 5:2 and 5:3 as "boast." Paul can then be understood as saying that we "boast" in the glory of God and even in our suffering. For earlier and related instances of the word "boast," see Romans 2:17, 23; and 3:27.

4. **B.**

   Abraham believed God's promise of an offspring despite his body, "which was as good as dead" (Rom. 4:19), which helps us understand what Paul means by the phrase about God "who gives life to the dead and calls into existence the things that do not exist" (v. 17). Dr. Godfrey made a connection to something that may have also been in Paul's mind and should certainly come to our minds: the creation of all things and the resurrection of Christ. The author of Hebrews, however, does connect Abraham's faith in God's power to raise the dead and the sacrifice of Isaac (see Heb. 11:17–19).

5. **A.**

   There are incidents in Abraham's life to which we can point to his weakness and doubt. Yet these incidents do not necessarily discount the genuineness of Abraham's faith. The fact that Abraham persevered through them is evidence of the strength of his faith such that Paul could say, "No unbelief made him waver concerning the promise of God" (Rom. 4:20).

6. **D.**

   Though we may grow in our love and our ability to love others through our suffering, Paul lists these as outcomes of our suffering in Christ: endurance, character, and hope (see Rom. 5:3–4).

9

Reconciliation & the Two Adams

INTRODUCTION

The reality of our reconciliation to God in Christ should astonish us. For all who have trusted in Christ, we are no longer "in Adam" but are now "in Christ," the second Adam. Once we were under the reign of death, but now we reign with Christ in life. In this lesson, Dr. Godfrey examines the glorious truth of reconciliation and why it was needed through exploring Paul's two-Adams theology in Romans 5.

LEARNING GOALS

When you have finished this lesson, you should be able to:

- Describe our condition when Christ came into the world to save us and appreciate His saving work in light of that condition
- Articulate the relationship between Adam and Christ as representatives or federal heads
- Define the active obedience and passive obedience of Christ

KEY IDEAS

- We are reconciled to God because of the life and death of Jesus Christ.
- There is a first Adam, who represents humanity as a federal head, and there is a second Adam, Jesus Christ, who likewise represents the redeemed of humanity as a federal head.
- Jesus' whole life was offered up to God as an act of obedience.

REFLECTION & DISCUSSION QUESTIONS

Before the Video

What Do You Think?

Take a moment to answer the following questions. They will prepare you for the lecture.

- Why is it remarkable that Christ died for you?

- How are Adam's sin and Christ's righteousness related? What makes them different?

Scripture Reading

Therefore, if anyone is in Christ, he is a new creation. The old has passed away; behold, the new has come. All this is from God, who through Christ reconciled us to himself and gave us the ministry of reconciliation; that is, in Christ God was reconciling the world to himself, not counting their trespasses against them, and entrusting to us the message of reconciliation. Therefore, we are ambassadors for Christ, God making his appeal through us. We implore you on behalf of Christ, be reconciled to God. For our sake he made him to be sin who knew no sin, so that in him we might become the righteousness of God.

—2 Corinthians 5:17–21

- According to this passage, what is one way that the truth of our reconciliation in Christ ought to work itself out practically in our lives?

During the Video

Answer the following questions while you watch the video. They will guide you through the lecture.

Reconciliation and the Origin of Sin *0:00–13:52*

- What is important to remember about our reconciliation to God not only through Christ's death but also through His life?

- In Paul's articulation of his two-Adams theology, why can it be said that our reconciliation to God in Christ is guaranteed?

Christ's Righteousness *13:52–24:53*

- What is the first interpretation of the phrase "one act of righteousness" (Rom. 5:18) that Dr. Godfrey introduced?
- What are the passive obedience and active obedience of Jesus Christ?
- What does Dr. Godfrey believe to be the correct interpretation of the phrase "one act of righteousness"?

After the Video

Answer the following questions after you have finished the lecture. They will help you identify and summarize the major points.

- Often, people resist the idea that we are all guilty of Adam's sin. Why is it important to affirm this truth in light of Adam's being "a type of the one who was to come" (Rom. 5:14)?

  If you are in a group, have the members read Romans 5:12–21. Ask: What all is contrasted with what was brought about by Adam's sin and what is brought about through Christ's righteousness?
- Why is Christ's active obedience critical for our salvation?

  If you are in a group, have the members identify what difference reflecting on the role of Christ's passive and active obedience for them can make in their daily lives. Ask: How can these two aspects of Christ's obedience affect how you feel, live, or process your sin?
- What are the possible interpretations of what Paul means by "all men" in Romans 5:18?

  If you are in a group, have the members read Romans 5:18–21 while keeping in mind what Dr. Godfrey said about Paul's preaching and how Paul will go on to address the charge of antinomianism. Ask: How can preaching exalt God's grace while not excusing sin?

PRAYER

Commit what you have learned from God's Word in this lesson to prayer.

- Praise God that He sent His Son into the world to pay the penalty for your sins.
- Confess ways that you fail to see your sin in view of its cost that Christ paid on the cross.
- Thank God for working through His covenants such that just as Adam's sin was made yours, so Christ's righteousness has been made yours.
- Ask God to help you rightly respond to His grace with a life of obedient gratitude in the Holy Spirit.

REVIEW QUIZ

Use these multiple-choice questions to measure what you learned from this lesson.

1. Romans 5 deals with which of the following?
   a. The universality of sin
   b. The seriousness of sin
   c. The repentance of sin
   d. The origin of sin

2. What does Paul's use of Old Testament figures in Romans demonstrate?
   a. That Jesus reshapes God's purpose in history.
   b. That Jesus creates a different people of God in the gentiles.
   c. That Jesus lays claim to the entirety of the Old Testament.
   d. That Jesus is a surprising answer to covenant infidelity.

3. What root word is prominent in Romans 5:12–21 as it relates to what Christ has accomplished?
   a. "Trespass"
   b. "Resurrect"
   c. "Justify"
   d. "Abound"

4. What document did Dr. Godfrey direct you to for further study on the covenants?
   a. Belgic Confession
   b. Canons of Dort
   c. Heidelberg Catechism
   d. Westminster Confession of Faith

5. Romans 5:18, stating that Christ's one act of righteousness leads to our justification, is a key proof text for Christ's passive obedience.
   a. True
   b. False

6. What is the overall tone of Paul's conclusion after reflecting on Adam and Christ in Romans 5?
   a. Academic
   b. Celebratory
   c. Encouraging
   d. Somber

Answer Key—Reconciliation & the Two Adams

REFLECTION & DISCUSSION QUESTIONS

Before the Video

What Do You Think?

These are personal questions. The answers should be based on your own knowledge and experience.

Scripture Reading

- According to this passage, what is one way that the truth of our reconciliation in Christ ought to work itself out practically in our lives?

  In this passage, the truth of our reconciliation to God in Christ is beautifully told; He has taken our sin and given us His righteousness. He has also given us "the ministry of reconciliation." Christians are called "ambassadors for Christ," so a practical way that the truth of our reconciliation works itself out in our lives is through our communicating this truth earnestly to others.

During the Video

Reconciliation and the Origin of Sin

- What is important to remember about our reconciliation to God not only through Christ's death but also through His life?

  In Romans 5:10, Paul says, "For if while we were enemies we were reconciled to God by the death of his Son, much more, now that we are reconciled, shall we be saved by his life." It is important to remember in reflecting on the death of Christ as the price of our reconciliation that He no longer remains dead. Just as He died for us, He now lives for us. We have not been abandoned or taken merely half the way there in the Christian life; Christ preserves us even now by His life.

- In Paul's articulation of his two-Adams theology, why can it be said that our reconciliation to God in Christ is guaranteed?

  As a federal head, Adam represented all humanity such that we are all guilty of his sin. In the same way, Christ stood in for the redeemed as a federal head such that He bore our penalty and we received His righteousness. Everyone is born "in Adam," but those who are "in Christ" have received the free gift of His righteousness, and because Paul describes this as a "free gift" of God (see Rom. 5:15–17), we can be sure that it is guaranteed, something solely dependent on Him and not us.

Christ's Righteousness

- What is the first interpretation of the phrase "one act of righteousness" (Rom. 5:18) that Dr. Godfrey introduced?

  Scholars and theologians raise an important question about what "one act of righteousness" Paul may be referring to. Some believe that this one act is the death of Jesus Christ, so Paul would be stressing Christ's obedience on the cross. But even this event is difficult to conceive of as "one act" of obedience, for many acts were involved in Christ's crucifixion, all of which He was obedient through.

- What are the passive and active obedience of Jesus Christ?

  Theologians make an important distinction between the passive and active obedience of Christ. The passive obedience of Christ is all that is involved in His submission to the cross to suffer on behalf of His people. The active obedience of Christ is His lifelong keeping of the law of God, which is also applied to our account.

- What does Dr. Godfrey believe to be the correct interpretation of the phrase "one act of righteousness"?

  Because it is difficult to conceive even of Christ's death on the cross as "one act," Dr. Godfrey offered another interpretation of the phrase "one act of obedience," connecting it to the whole of Christ's life. In other words, this one act is Christ's active obedience in its entirety. Christ's whole life, from His birth to His ascension, was one act of obedience and service to God.

After the Video

- Often, people resist the idea that we are all guilty of Adam's sin. Why is it important to affirm this truth in light of Adam's being "a type of the one who was to come" (Rom. 5:14)?

  In Romans 5:14, Paul calls Adam "a type of the one who was to come." When Adam sinned, we all sinned because he was our federal head in the covenant of works. This is half of Paul's two-Adams theology. The other half is the glorious truth that Christ is the federal head of the covenant of grace. We must affirm Adam's representative headship so that we might also affirm Christ's representative headship. We cannot have one without the other.

- Why is Christ's active obedience critical for our salvation?

  In His passive obedience, Jesus suffered and died for our sins, that they might be covered. In Christ, we can no longer be condemned for our sins. But God does not leave us there. God credits to our account the active obedience of Jesus Christ, which means that we receive His righteous standing in keeping all the law of God. We not only stand before God as guiltless, but because of the active obedience of Christ, we also stand before Him as righteous.

- What are the possible interpretations of what Paul means by "all men" in Romans 5:18?

  Of many interpretations, one would understand Paul as espousing universalism, that Christ's obedience has led to justification for "all men." There are other ways of understanding this phrase, however, that do not contradict Paul's teaching elsewhere. Dr. Godfrey proposed that Paul may be speaking hyperbolically and with great enthusiasm about the effects brought about by Christ's death and righteousness. When we understand this verse in light of Paul's two-Adams theology, he is saying that "all" who are in Adam die, but that "all" who are in Christ are justified. If not understood in this way, it would seem that Paul immediately contradicts himself. In Romans 5:19, he says, "For as by the one man's disobedience the many *were made sinners, so by the one man's obedience the* many *will be made righteous" (emphasis added). The "many" are not "all."*

REVIEW QUIZ

1. **D.**
   Earlier in Romans 2–3, Paul dealt with the seriousness and universality of sin. In Romans 5, he traces sin back to its origin, all the way back to Adam's trespass in the garden.
2. **C.**
   Dr. Godfrey said, "Jesus makes His claim on the whole of the Old Testament," in response to Paul's tracing Christ back to David, Abraham, and Adam. Jesus and His ministry should not have taken God's people by surprise. God was not doing anything different through Christ from what had already been planned.
3. **D.**
   Though the word "trespass" occurs many times, it connects to Adam's sin. While the word "justify" relates to what Christ accomplished, it occurs only once. Dr. Godfrey did note, however, that Paul uses some form of the word "abound" three times in Romans 5 to emphasize the lavishness of what Christ has given to us (vv. 15, 17, 20).
4. **D.**
   Each of these documents would be a rich resource for further study in the Reformed heritage. Dr. Godfrey directed further study on covenant theology, particularly, to chapter 7 of the Westminster Confession of Faith, which is titled "Of God's Covenant with Man."
5. **B.**
   Christ's passive obedience largely relates to His suffering and death on behalf of our sins. Christ's active obedience relates to His obedience to God's law through the whole of His life. Dr. Godfrey argued for interpreting the "one act of righteousness" in Romans 5:18 as referring to the whole of Christ's life of active obedience to God.

6. **B.**
   While encouragement ought to flow naturally from any extended reflection on the grace of God that has been abundantly given to us in Jesus Christ, Dr. Godfrey suggested that Paul's tone at the end of Romans 5 is celebratory. This celebration of grace is doxological in many ways.

10

New Identity in Christ

INTRODUCTION

Christians are no longer dead in their sin but have been made newly alive unto righteousness in Jesus Christ. This reality of who we are ought to inform how we live, which is the fundamental lesson that Paul teaches us in Romans 6:1–14. In this lesson, Dr. Godfrey transitions into a new section of Paul's letter that focuses on how we live out our salvation in Christ.

LEARNING GOALS

When you have finished this lesson, you should be able to:

- Understand the unified argument of Romans 6–8
- Articulate the criticism being raised against Paul in Romans 6 and how he responds
- Define an essential feature at the beginning of the process of sanctification

KEY IDEAS

- Knowing who we are in Christ first helps us to live out the Christian life.
- The essential identity of the Christian is that we have died to sin and are alive to Christ.
- Sanctification is the battle that goes on between who we are essentially in Christ and the remnants of the flesh.

REFLECTION & DISCUSSION QUESTIONS

Before the Video

What Do You Think?

Take a moment to answer the following questions. They will prepare you for the lecture.

- Why is sanctification an important part of the Christian life?

- What are some ways that we can misunderstand sanctification?

Scripture Reading

> *For we ourselves were once foolish, disobedient, led astray, slaves to various passions and pleasures, passing our days in malice and envy, hated by others and hating one another. But when the goodness and loving kindness of God our Savior appeared, he saved us, not because of works done by us in righteousness, but according to his own mercy, by the washing of regeneration and renewal of the Holy Spirit, whom he poured out on us richly through Jesus Christ our Savior, so that being justified by his grace we might become heirs according to the hope of eternal life.*
>
> —Titus 3:3–7

- Who were you before coming to know Christ? Who are you now?

During the Video

Answer the following questions while you watch the video. They will guide you through the lecture.

The Central Section *0:00–9:52*

- What does the central section of the book of Romans deal with?

- What is one way that sanctification has been misunderstood in the history of the church? What does Paul teach about sanctification in Romans 6:1–14?

Dead to Sin and Alive in Christ *9:52–18:58*

- How does Paul answer the criticism that he is indifferent to sin in Romans 6?

- How does Paul speak about the significance of baptism in Romans 6?

The Mortal Body *18:58–25:25*

- Why does Paul mention the "mortal body" (Rom. 6:12)?

After the Video

Answer the following questions after you have finished the lecture. They will help you identify and summarize the major points.

- What is one way to misunderstand what Paul is teaching in phrases such as "set free from sin" and "dead to sin" (Rom. 6:7, 11)? What do such misinterpretations teach us about studying the Bible?

  If you are in a group, have the members bring to mind passages that they have misunderstood or misread out of context and discuss how their minds were changed about the meaning of these passages.

- In what ways does the New Testament picture baptism as being brought from death to life?

  If you are in a group, have the members discuss how they ought to reflect on their baptism. Ask: What ought we to think about when we see someone getting baptized?

- Does sin reside in the body? Explain. What must we remember to not let sin reign in our mortal bodies?

  If you are in a group, have the members discuss how reflecting on their identity in Christ can affect their daily interactions with others and with themselves. Ask: How does your new identity in Christ teach you to deal with personal conflict or guilt and shame?

PRAYER

Commit what you have learned from God's Word in this lesson to prayer.

- Praise God for the life and death of His Son, to whom you are united by faith.
- Confess any sins, particularly those that are committed through your body, that you tolerate.
- Thank God for your new identity in Jesus Christ, that you are now dead to sin and alive to righteousness, just as He died for your sins and was raised for your justification (Rom. 4:25).

- Ask God to enable you to live out the resurrection life of the Christian through the power of the Holy Spirit so that sin no longer reigns in your mortal body.

REVIEW QUIZ

Use these multiple-choice questions to measure what you learned from this lesson.

1. Romans 6:1–8:39 can be understood under which of the following section titles?
   a. "Salvation Assured"
   b. "Salvation Experienced"
   c. "Salvation Needed"
   d. "Salvation Provided"

2. In Romans 6:1–8:39, Paul addresses false accusations related to which of the following?
   a. Sacraments
   b. Interpretation of the Old Testament
   c. Jew-gentile relationships
   d. Antinomianism

3. Which of the following are *not* connected to baptism in the New Testament?
   a. Abraham's journey in Egypt
   b. Christ's burial and resurrection
   c. Israel's crossing through the Red Sea
   d. Noah's salvation through the flood

4. The flow of Paul's thought in Romans 6:1–14 helps us to see which of the following?
   a. The heart of the Apostle for his fellow Israelites
   b. The importance of the Holy Spirit in sanctification
   c. The literary unity of Romans 6–8 as an entire section
   d. The main point of Romans through a chiastic structure

5. Our progress in sanctification establishes our identity.
   a. True
   b. False

6. Which of the following inaccurately describes the theology that was taught by Dr. Godfrey as it relates to the phrase "mortal body"?
   a. There is a constant battle with sin in the Christian life.
   b. There is a reality of remaining sin that the body testifies to.
   c. There is an essential self that is different from our outer self.
   d. There is an absolute sinfulness to our physical bodies.

Answer Key—New Identity in Christ

REFLECTION & DISCUSSION QUESTIONS

Before the Video

What Do You Think?

These are personal questions. The answers should be based on your own knowledge and experience.

Scripture Reading

- Who were you before coming to know Christ? Who are you now?

  This passage uses very strong language to help us to understand who we were apart from God's grace. Whether our lives were marked by foolishness or a slavery to our passions, we were in need of God's mercy. In Christ, we have been washed and renewed by the Holy Spirit and justified before God. In addition to this, we rejoice in the staggering truth that we are now heirs of eternal life.

During the Video

The Central Section

- What does the central section of the book of Romans deal with?

  This central section of Paul's letter deals with matters of sanctification. We should not be surprised that this topic is positioned so centrally in the letter because throughout Romans, Paul has been addressing accusations that he does not understand the nature of the Christian life, particularly in relation to the law. In Romans 6:1–8:39, Paul is ready to expound on his understanding of how to live out our salvation in Christ.

- What is one way that sanctification has been misunderstood in the history of the church? What does Paul teach about sanctification in Romans 6:1–14?

  One major error about sanctification in church history is the belief that our salvation hangs in the balance based on our sanctification. This has been taught by both Arminians and Roman Catholics. Even in Reformed circles, we may nuance sanctification in the wrong ways, perhaps suggesting that we need only to try harder in the Christian life. In Romans 6:1–14, Paul teaches that sanctification is lived out of our new identity in Christ. We must know who we are in order to properly live out the Christian life, a process that is not perfect but through which we will ultimately triumph.

Dead to Sin and Alive in Christ

- How does Paul answer the criticism that he is indifferent to sin in Romans 6?

  Paul asks a number of questions to challenge the criticism that he was facing head on. In his emphasis on grace, many thought Paul was ignoring the role of God's law in the Christian life, as though he were promoting sin so that grace may abound. Paul's questions in the beginning of Romans 6 show how absurd such an idea is. He asks, "How can we who died to sin still live in it?" (v. 2). What Paul has been accused of teaching is completely inconsistent with the new identity of the Christian life—we have died to sin.

- How does Paul speak about the significance of baptism in Romans 6?

  As a sign of the new covenant, baptism points to many realities. For instance, it can point to the cleansing of our sin and guilt. In Romans 6, Paul explains the significance of baptism in another: as a sign of being buried with Christ and raised with Him in newness of life (see v. 4). This baptism should inform the identity out of which we live the Christian life.

The Mortal Body

- Why does Paul mention the "mortal body" (Rom. 6:12)?

  Not stressing some sort of mind-body dualism, Paul mentions our "mortal bodies" in contrast to our being alive in Christ. As we live out the Christian life, our bodies are the best reminders to us that our lives are mortal and dying away and that sin is still a reality that we must deal with. Paul's mention of "mortal body" may allude to Abraham (see Rom. 4:19), and this should remind us to maintain faith throughout our struggles against sin, knowing that God has already raised us in our union with Christ.

After the Video

- What is one way to misunderstand what Paul is teaching in phrases such as "set free from sin" and "dead to sin" (Rom. 6:7, 11)? What do such misinterpretations teach us about studying the Bible?

  Such phrases have been used to suggest that Paul teaches a form of perfectionism, that Christians can attain a state of sinlessness because they are entirely free from sin. Paul teaches that Christians are set free and dead to sin, indeed, but he does not teach perfectionism. The context that surrounds these phrases shows that Paul acknowledges that there will be difficulty with sin in the Christian life. This reinforces for us the importance of studying the Bible with the context of any given passage in mind so that we do not rip it out of context and jeopardize its intended meaning.

- In what ways does the New Testament picture baptism as being brought from death to life?

  In addition to baptism's being a sign of cleansing, it is also spoken of in the New Testament as a sign of passing through death and judgment into life. Paul pictures this through the burial and resurrection of Jesus Christ in Romans 6:4. In other places in the New Testament, different pictures are used. In 1 Peter 3, baptism is likened to Noah's being saved with his family through the waters of death in the flood (vv. 18–22). In 1 Corinthians 10, Paul speaks about the Israelites as being "baptized into Moses" and alludes to the Red Sea, through which the Israelites passed and lived.

- Does sin reside in the body? Explain. What must we remember to not let sin reign in our mortal bodies?

  Sin is not particular only to our bodies. It is not as if we are free from sin only in our souls or spirits and must wage war against our sinful bodies. Yet our bodies are one of the most pronounced reminders that sin is still present to us as we live out life bodily in this fallen world. In another sense, there is an inner aspect about us, a true identity or essential self in Christ, that speaks to the reality that we have been changed. We are dead to sin and alive to Jesus Christ, and this is what we must remember so that sin does not reign in our mortal bodies (see Rom. 6:12–14; 1 Peter 2:11).

REVIEW QUIZ

1. **B.**

   "Salvation Experienced" or "Salvation Lived" is the fourth major section of Paul's letter, coming after the letter's introduction (Rom. 1:1–17), "Salvation Needed" (1:18–3:20), and "Salvation Provided" (3:21–5:21).

2. **D.**

   Though Paul does tie baptism to our central identity as those who have died to sin and have been made alive to Christ, Romans 6:1–8:39 largely deals with sanctification. Thus, it connects to the false accusations that Paul addressed earlier in the letter that his emphasis on the grace of God was a promotion of lawlessness or antinomianism (see Rom. 3:8; 6:1–3).

3. **A.**

   Paul connects baptism to Jesus' burial and resurrection in Romans 6:4 and to the Israelites' being baptized into Moses in the "sea" in 1 Corinthians 10:1–2. Peter also connects baptism to Noah's salvation through the waters of the flood. Each of these events communicates something about what baptism brings us through—namely, death. Though Abraham's journey in Egypt anticipates Israel's time in Egypt and subsequent exodus, it is not connected to baptism in the New Testament.

4. **C.**
Although Romans 6:1–8:39 can be understood as the central part of the letter, 6:1–14 is not itself a chiasm. This passage does, however, give us an excellent insight into the essential unity of Romans 6–8. The Word of God was not received with chapters and verses, and these features in our Bibles can sometimes obscure the unity of a passage or even an entire book. Romans 6:1–14 states the topics that Paul will address in the same order throughout chapter 8.

5. **B.**
Paul describes our identity as those who are now dead to sin and alive to God in Jesus Christ. It is from this identity that we press on in our sanctification. Our progress in sanctification, in this sense, does not define who we are in Christ, but how we understand our identity in Christ can dramatically shape our growth in grace.

6. **D.**
While the Bible clearly speaks of an antagonism between the Spirit and flesh (Gal. 5:16–24), it does not teach us that the body itself is absolutely sinful. A warfare against sin is made visible to us in the body, but sin is not physical; it does not reside in the body.

11

The Ongoing Struggle

INTRODUCTION

Christians have radical new identity in Christ, and though our battle with sin continues, we know that sin no longer has dominion over us. This is the fundamental message of Paul's teaching in Romans 6–7. In this lesson, Dr. Godfrey gives us hope in our ongoing struggle against sin in the Christian life by focusing our attention on the Apostle Paul's own testimony in the much-debated passage of Romans 7.

LEARNING GOALS

When you have finished this lesson, you should be able to:

- Recognize a key signpost of sanctification in the Christian life
- Describe the alternative interpretations of Paul's experience in Romans 7
- Formulate your own position on Paul's experience in Romans 7

KEY IDEAS

- Sin cannot have mastery over the Christian because we are now dead to sin and alive to Christ, having been purchased by a new Master to live as slaves unto righteousness.
- Sanctification, while not the means of earning salvation, can be directly connected to eternal life in Scripture because it is the process that everyone who has eternal life experiences.
- The flow of Paul's argument lends itself to the historically Calvinist interpretation of Romans 7 that Paul is describing his struggle with sin as a Christian.

REFLECTION & DISCUSSION QUESTIONS

Before the Video

What Do You Think?

Take a moment to answer the following questions. They will prepare you for the lecture.

- What does it feel like to struggle with sin?

- Why is it sometimes hard to measure your growth in sanctification?

Scripture Reading

Now may the God of peace himself sanctify you completely, and may your whole spirit and soul and body be kept blameless at the coming of our Lord Jesus Christ. He who calls you is faithful; he will surely do it.

—1 Thessalonians 5:23–24

- What does this benediction in 1 Thessalonians teach us about sanctification?

During the Video

Answer the following questions while you watch the video. They will guide you through the lecture.

On the Way to Eternal Life *0:00–8:40*

- What are the three points that Paul summarizes in Romans 6:1–14 that are elaborated on throughout Romans 6–8?

- What does Paul mean when he says that the end of sanctification is eternal life (Rom. 6:22)? What can't he mean?

Paul's Struggle *8:40–18:24*

- What is the traditional Calvinist interpretation of Romans 7?

- What is the Arminian interpretation of Romans 7? What's the basis for this interpretation?

Answering Difficulties *18:24–24:52*

- How can we explain Paul's statement that "I was once alive apart from the law" in line with the Calvinist interpretation of Romans 7?

- Is it necessary to conclude that Paul is referring to a time before he was a Christian when he says that he is "of the flesh"?

After the Video

Answer the following questions after you have finished the lecture. They will help you identify and summarize the major points.

- In what sense can the Christian life be discouraging as it relates to sanctification?

  If you are in a group, have the members describe ways in which they can positively see evidence of their sanctification in the Christian life.

- How do you interpret Paul's experience in Romans 7—as describing his life as a Christian or before he became a Christian? How do you relate to Paul's experience?

  If you are in a group, have the members read Romans 6 and explain what phrases in Romans 7 challenge the traditional Calvinist interpretation of Romans 7 and why. Ask: What passages in Romans 7 nonetheless support this interpretation?

- What is Paul's understanding of the law up to this point in Romans? What is his point in contrasting the new way of the Spirit and the old way of the law?

  If you are in a group, have the members read Romans 7:1–6 and discuss how Paul's analogy fits with his argument about the Christian's relationship to the law.

PRAYER

Commit what you have learned from God's Word in this lesson to prayer.

- Praise God for the work of Jesus Christ in liberating a people for Himself.

- Confess ways that you fall back into living as if you were still a slave to sin.
- Thank God that you have been delivered from the impossible task of seeking a righteousness through the law.
- Ask God by the Holy Spirit to help you put your sin to death in union with Jesus Christ, who died for your sins in His body on the cross.

REVIEW QUIZ

Use these multiple-choice questions to measure what you learned from this lesson.

1. What echo did Dr. Godfrey connect to Paul's primary metaphor in Romans 6?
   a. "Paul, a servant of Christ Jesus" (Rom. 1:1)
   b. "O man—you who judge" (2:3)
   c. "The father of all who believe" (4:11)
   d. "Baptized into Christ Jesus" (6:3)

2. Paul warmly refers to the Romans as "brothers" again in Romans 7.
   a. True
   b. False

3. Which theologian did Dr. Godfrey reference to explain how closely Paul connects sanctification with eternal life?
   a. Herman Ridderbos
   b. Jacobus Arminius
   c. John Calvin
   d. Martin Luther

4. Some interpreters suggest that Paul is not always speaking about himself when he uses the word "I" because it is hard to conceive of a time when Paul, a Pharisee, was "apart from the law," for instance.
   a. True
   b. False

5. Which theologian disagrees with the position taken on Romans 7 by Dr. Godfrey?
   a. Herman Ridderbos
   b. Jacobus Arminius
   c. John Calvin
   d. Both a and b

6. Which of the following presents the most difficulty to the traditionally Calvinist interpretation of Romans 7?
   a. "I agree with the law" (Rom. 7:16).
   b. "I am of the flesh, sold under sin" (7:14).
   c. "I delight in the law of God" (7:22).
   d. "I do the very thing I hate" (7:15).

Answer Key—The Ongoing Struggle

REFLECTION & DISCUSSION QUESTIONS

Before the Video

What Do You Think?

These are personal questions. The answers should be based on your own knowledge and experience.

Scripture Reading

- What does this benediction in 1 Thessalonians teach us about sanctification?

  Often when we think about our sanctification, we can mistakenly believe that it is entirely up to us, but in this benediction, Paul pronounces the blessing that "God . . . himself" would do this work and do it "completely." We see also that sanctification is a process that occurs throughout our entire Christian lives to preserve us until the day of Christ Jesus, at which time our sanctification will be made perfect. We can be sure that "God . . . himself" is faithful to do this.

During the Video

On the Way to Eternal Life

- What are the three points that Paul summarizes in Romans 6:1–14 that are elaborated on throughout Romans 6–8?

  By way of review, the first two points are that we must know our identity in Christ ("Know who you are") and that we must labor against sin on the foundation of this identity ("Live out your new life"). The final point introduced in this lesson is that sin will have no dominion over us, that we will ultimately win the battle against sin in the Christian life.

- What does Paul mean when he says that the end of sanctification is eternal life (Rom. 6:22)? What can't he mean?

  One might read this phrase in Romans 6:22 that the end of sanctification is eternal life and believe that some measure of sanctification must be achieved to attain eternal life. In one sense, sanctification is necessary for salvation, but not as something that earns or merits salvation. All who have the "free gift" of eternal life are being sanctified (v. 23), such that Scripture can closely equate sanctification and eternal life to such a degree that they are two sides of the same coin.

Paul's Struggle

- What is the traditional Calvinist interpretation of Romans 7?

  In Romans 7, Paul can be referring, among other things, to his experience with the law and sin as it was before becoming a Christian or as a Christian. The traditional Calvinist interpretation is that Paul is describing his real struggles with sin as a Christian.

- What is the Arminian interpretation of Romans 7? What's the basis for this interpretation?

  Jacobus Arminius was a Dutch theologian who challenged key tenets of the biblical Reformed faith. He did not believe that Paul could say the words "I am of the flesh, sold under sin" as a Christian (Rom. 7:14). He concluded, therefore, that Paul must be speaking in Romans 7 from a preconversion perspective.

Answering Difficulties

- How can we explain Paul's statement that "I was once alive apart from the law" in line with the Calvinist interpretation of Romans 7?

  Paul's statement is challenging and leads interpreters to assume that Paul must no longer be talking about himself and using "I" as some rhetorical device. But there is a way of understanding how Paul, someone who was raised as a Jew with deep familiarity with the law, could say that he was once alive apart from it. As a Pharisee, Paul believed that a righteousness through the law was attainable and did not understand that the law was intended to teach him that he was a sinner. So Paul could be familiar with the law yet not comprehend the essential message of the law.

- Is it necessary to conclude that Paul is referring to a time before he was a Christian when he says that he is "of the flesh"?

  While such phrases as "of the flesh" and "sold under sin" are strong language (Rom. 7:14), Paul does use the term "flesh" even to refer to Christians elsewhere. One example of this is in his first letter to the Corinthians, where he says: "I fed you with milk, not solid food, for you were not ready for it. And even now you are not yet ready, for you are still of the flesh. For while there is jealousy and strife among you, are you not of the flesh and behaving only in a human way?" (1 Cor. 3:2–3). It is therefore not necessary to conclude that Paul is referring to himself before he was a Christian in saying that he is "of the flesh."

After the Video

- In what sense can the Christian life be discouraging as it relates to sanctification?

  Sanctification is a process that every Christian experiences. The fact that it is a process and not instantaneous can be frustrating in itself. The reason is that, as Christians, we no longer love our sin. In fact, we can get discouraged in the sanctification process because we come to recognize our sin more and more even as we grow in holiness and our longing be Christlike. While this seems discouraging, we can also look at this reality as evidence of our sanctification, and in this sense, our great struggle against sin can become an encouragement to us.

- How do you interpret Paul's experience in Romans 7—as describing his life as a Christian or before he became a Christian? How do you relate to Paul's experience?

  This question requires you to state a position on Paul's experience in Romans 7, taking into consideration the points of contention between the Arminian and traditionally Calvinist positions. Additionally, the second question requires a sober look at your struggle with sin, regardless of how you interpret Romans 7.

- What is Paul's understanding of the law up to this point in Romans? What is his point in contrasting the new way of the Spirit and the old way of the law?

  Up to this point in Romans, Paul has stressed the inability of the law to bring about a righteousness that would be sufficient for our salvation. Law-keeping is unable to save us, and the law itself is intended to show us how far we fall short of keeping it, exposing us to our sin. For Paul, this does not mean that the law is sinful or unholy, as he appears to have been accused of teaching. Rather, the law is holy and spiritual, and it is our own sinful nature that explains its powerlessness to save. This is why Paul contrasts the new way of the Spirit with the old way of the law. It is not as if the law is meaningless to us now, but the Spirit who gives life releases us from the condemnation of the law and attempting to attain righteousness through the law.

REVIEW QUIZ

1. **A.**
   Our relationship to the law and our relationship to Christ are likened to the relationship between a master and a slave in Romans 6, which echoes Paul's opening words in this letter: "Paul, a servant of Christ Jesus" (Rom. 1:1).

2. **A.**
   Paul addresses the Roman Christians in a very fraternal, intimate, family kind of way. In the struggle of the Christian life, Paul thinks of these Christians as brothers, confident that they have understood the gospel and will understand the points he has been making about sanctification.

3. **C.**
   Dr. Godfrey underscored the helpfulness of John Calvin in explaining the close-knit relationship between sanctification and eternal life. It is not that sanctification

earns eternal life, but all those who have eternal life go through the process of sanctification such that eternal life can be called its "end" (see Rom. 6:22).

4. **A.**
Some do find it difficult to explain such phrases as Paul's being "apart from the law," for he was taught the law as a child and became a Pharisee. For this reason, they argue that Paul may be using a rhetorical technique to refer to an entity other than himself, yet we can conceive of how it would be possible for Paul to have been "apart from the law" if, as a Pharisee, he saw it only as a means to righteousness and not as a mirror of his sin.

5. **D.**
Though Herman Ridderbos is a Calvinist and not an Arminian, this Dutch theologian disagrees with the traditional Calvinist interpretation of Romans 7 that Paul is describing his struggle with sin as a Christian.

6. **B.**
Of all these choices, the one that is most difficult to apply to a Christian concerns being in the flesh, in slavery under sin. We would easily say, however, that an agreement with, a delight in, and a desire to do God's law are in full accord with what it is to be a Christian.

12

Assured of Salvation, Alive in the Spirit

INTRODUCTION

Assured of our identity in Christ, we are called to struggle against sin, and we are enabled to do so because we have been made alive through the Holy Spirit. Not only do we see this reality played out in our own lives, but we also see it as it was played out in the life of the Apostle Paul in Romans 7. In this lesson, Dr. Godfrey continues his defense of the Calvinist interpretation of Romans 7 and demonstrates how Romans 8 is intimately connected to Romans 7, giving us hope in our struggle against sin in the knowledge that we are adopted sons and daughters of God.

LEARNING GOALS

When you have finished this lesson, you should be able to:

- Understand and explain how Romans 8 is the answer to the struggle of Romans 7
- Articulate how there is no longer any condemnation for those in Christ (Rom. 8:1)

KEY IDEAS

- Christians' struggle with sin is an ongoing, lawlike reality that will one day end when we are fully delivered by Jesus Christ.
- The degree to which we struggle or experience victory in our struggle against sin is not determinative of our freedom from condemnation.
- In Christ, we are made alive in the Spirit and thus given hope and encouragement in our struggle against sin.

REFLECTION & DISCUSSION QUESTIONS

Before the Video

What Do You Think?

Take a moment to answer the following questions. They will prepare you for the lecture.

- Why is Romans 8 such a beloved chapter of the Bible?
- Why do you continue in the struggle against sin as a Christian?

Scripture Reading

I will sprinkle clean water on you, and you shall be clean from all your uncleannesses, and from all your idols I will cleanse you. And I will give you a new heart, and a new spirit I will put within you. And I will remove the heart of stone from your flesh and give you a heart of flesh. And I will put my Spirit within you, and cause you to walk in my statutes and be careful to obey my rules.

—Ezekiel 36:25–27

- What does the Spirit-filled life include, according to this passage?

During the Video

Answer the following questions while you watch the video. They will guide you through the lecture.

The Struggle against Sin *0:00–8:18*

- What does Paul's statement "I do the very thing I hate" in Romans 7:15 suggest about the type of experience that he is describing throughout Romans 7?
- What does Paul mean by the word "law" in Romans 7:21?
- What meaning is behind Paul's question "Who will deliver me from this body of death?" in Romans 7:24?

The Answer of Romans 8 *8:18–23:46*

- What is significant about Paul's use of the word "now" in Romans 8:1?
- What major contrast does Paul make to life in the Spirit? What do these two lives lead to?

After the Video

Answer the following questions after you have finished the lecture. They will help you identify and summarize the major points.

- Is Paul excusing sin in his statements such as "Now if I do what I do not want, it is no longer I who do it, but sin that dwells within me" (Rom. 7:20)? Explain.

  If you are in a group, have the members discuss the reasons that they support a particular interpretation of Romans 7. Ask: Should our Christian experience govern our interpretation of a passage or be used only to support it?
- In what ways does Romans 8 connect with the preceding chapters in Paul's letter?

  If you are in a group, have the members review Romans 6:1–14 and identify how all its themes are present in Romans 6:15–23; 7; 8.
- What should Paul's contrast between the flesh and the Spirit cause us to think or do?

  If you are in a group, have the members consider and discuss the questions that Dr. Godfrey asked at the end of this lecture, such as "Do you love to go to church?" and "Do you see the fruit of the Spirit in your life?"

PRAYER

Commit what you have learned from God's Word in this lesson to prayer.

- Praise God for your freedom in the Spirit.
- Confess any ways that you are overcome by the things of the flesh.
- Thank God that He has promised to complete the work of your sanctification as assuredly as you have been justified in Jesus Christ.
- Ask God to continue to give you assurance through the Holy Spirit in your struggle against sin and even tangible growth in the areas in which you particularly struggle.

REVIEW QUIZ

Use these multiple-choice questions to measure what you learned from this lesson.

1. Which of the following lines from Romans 6 is expanded on in Romans 8?
   a. "Do not present your members to sin as instruments for unrighteousness" (v. 13).
   b. "Let not sin therefore reign in your mortal body, to make you obey its passions" (v. 12).
   c. "Present yourselves to God as those who have been brought from death to life" (v. 13).
   d. "Sin will have no dominion over you" (v. 14).

2. Dr. Godfrey holds that the Calvinist interpretation of Romans 7 is "right." What other alliterative quality does Dr. Godfrey connect to this interpretation of Romans 7?
   a. Rich
   b. Radiant
   c. Relevant
   d. Resonant

3. What is the summary statement of Romans 7?
   a. "I delight in the law of God, in my inner being" (v. 22).
   b. "I myself serve the law of God with my mind, but with my flesh I serve the law of sin" (v. 25).
   c. "The evil I do not want is what I keep on doing" (v. 19).
   d. "Wretched man that I am! Who will deliver me from this body of death?" (v. 24).

4. Which of the following is *not* one of the four parts of Romans 8 as outlined by Dr. Godfrey?
   a. Abiding in Christ
   b. Adopted as Sons
   c. Alive in the Spirit
   d. Assured of Salvation

5. Romans 8 is longer than Romans 6 but shorter than Romans 7.
   a. True
   b. False

6. What is the primary doctrinal matter in Paul's view in the opening verses of Romans 8 when he talks about our walking in righteousness?
   a. Adoption
   b. Glorification
   c. Justification
   d. Sanctification

Answer Key—Assured of Salvation, Alive in the Spirit

REFLECTION & DISCUSSION QUESTIONS

Before the Video

What Do You Think?

These are personal questions. The answers should be based on your own knowledge and experience.

Scripture Reading

- What does the Spirit-filled life include, according to this passage?

  In addition to being cleansed and given a new heart, those who are indwelt by the Spirit walk in obedience to the law of God. This obedience is not done to gain a righteousness of our own but is a reality of the Spirit's work within us. Far from teaching antinomianism as he was accused of doing, Paul expands on this reality in Romans 8.

During the Video

The Struggle against Sin

- What does Paul's statement "I do the very thing I hate" in Romans 7:15 suggest about the type of experience that he is describing throughout Romans 7?

  John Calvin observed that an unregenerate person cannot speak this way about his or her sin. People cannot hate sin when they love it. This statement would be inconsistent were Paul describing a preconversion experience. Therefore, Paul is describing his experience and struggle against sin as a believer.

- What does Paul mean by the word "law" in Romans 7:21?

  In Romans 7:21, Paul says, "So I find it to be a law that when I want to do right, evil lies close at hand." By using the word "law," Paul forces us to slow down and think, because he is not referring to the Mosaic law here. He is referring to an ongoing reality of the Christian life that is consistent and recurring enough that it can be called a "law."

- What meaning is behind Paul's question "Who will deliver me from this body of death?" in Romans 7:24?

  Often, this question is read as though Paul were saying, "Who will save me?" This is especially so because it follows Paul's pronouncement that he is a "wretched man." But Paul is describing his experience as a Christian and calling himself "wretched" in relation to his struggle against sin, which is a wretched thing. The meaning of Paul's question, then, is not "Who will save me?" but "Who will sanctify me?"

The Answer of Romans 8

- What is significant about Paul's use of the word "now" in Romans 8:1?

  Dr. Godfrey underscored that Paul's use of the word "now" in Romans 8:1 assures us that our struggle against sin is not determinative of our being free from condemnation. Jesus Christ is the One who has freed us from condemnation. We are no longer under the condemnation of the law because He has taken our condemnation upon Himself.

- What major contrast does Paul make to life in the Spirit? What do these two lives lead to?

  Similar to the contrast that was made between our being a slave to sin and being a slave to righteousness, Paul contrasts life in the Spirit with life in the flesh. Life in the flesh is marked by setting our minds on the things of the flesh, which leads to sin and death. Life in the Spirit, on the other hand, leads to life and peace.

After the Video

- Is Paul excusing sin in his statements such as "Now if I do what I do not want, it is no longer I who do it, but sin that dwells within me" (Rom. 7:20)? Explain.

  Though Paul says that the sin within him causes him to sin, he is not excusing his sin. Paul would not be so emotionally distraught about deliverance if that were the case (see Rom. 7:24–25). Rather, Paul is elaborating on the warfare between the flesh and the Spirit that he described earlier in Romans 6–7. He is contrasting his essential self with the remaining sin that is communicated in terms such as "mortal body," "flesh," and "members."

- In what ways does Romans 8 connect with the preceding chapters in Paul's letter?

  Romans 8 is an expansion of Paul's statement in Romans 6:14, "For sin will have no dominion over you, since you are not under law but under grace." It follows Romans 7, which is Paul's description of the turmoil that Christians can experience in struggling against sin, as an encouragement that we will not ultimately be defeated in this struggle. Understood this way, Romans 8 gives us the assurance that sin will not have dominion over us and that the Spirit will supply what we need to persevere.

- What should Paul's contrast between the flesh and the Spirit cause us to think or do?

  The answers to this question may vary. In the context and overall purpose of Romans 8 to proclaim the rich truths of sanctification by the Spirit, it ought to encourage us and enliven us to be diligent in our struggle against sin. One of the ways that Dr. Godfrey applied Paul's contrast was to prompt us to personal reflection. When Paul contrasts life in the flesh and life in the Spirit, it is natural for us to ask which of these lives we are living. We ought to see the evidence of the Spirit's work in our lives, for we have been made different people by the work of the Spirit.

REVIEW QUIZ

1. **D.**
   Dr. Godfrey has argued that Romans 6:1–14 acts almost like a thesis for Romans 6–8. He specifically connected the struggle captured in 6:12–13 with Romans 7 and the assurance of 6:14 with Romans 8.

2. **D.**
   Dr. Godfrey holds to the conviction that the historic Calvinist interpretation of Romans 7 that Paul is describing his experience with sin as a Christian is right, and he also believes that it is resonant. As Christians, we can recognize something of our own experience in Paul's struggle.

3. **B.**
   Each of these statements can be used to stress the tension of Romans 7. On the one hand, Paul is a Christian, as can be seen in his love for the law of God and desire to pursue righteousness. On the other hand, he still struggles with sin. Dr. Godfrey pointed to Romans 7:25, the last verse of the chapter, as a summary statement of what Paul has been describing throughout Romans 7: "I myself serve the law of God with my mind, but with my flesh I serve the law of sin."

4. **A.**
   Though Christ is the reason that Christians know that there is no longer condemnation (Rom. 8:1), "Abiding in Christ" was not delineated as a section of Romans 8. "Assured of Salvation" (vv. 1–4), "Alive in the Spirit" (vv. 5–13), "Adopted as Sons" (vv. 14–27), and "Assured of Perseverance" (vv. 28–39) were the section titles given for Romans 8.

5. **B.**
   Romans 8 is longer than both Romans 6 and 7. This should be a great encouragement to us, that the battle with sin that is described in Romans 6–7 is given a shorter treatment than our assurance of ultimate victory in Romans 8.

6. **D.**
   Paul deals with each of these doctrines in Romans 8, but when he refers to our walking in righteousness—even that "the righteous requirement of the law might be fulfilled in us" (Rom. 8:4)—he has our sanctification in view, as argued by Dr. Godfrey.

13

Adopted as Sons

INTRODUCTION

Romans 8 expands on Paul's earlier promise that sin will have no dominion over us who are in Christ (6:1–2). It is a rich chapter of assurance, and this assurance is rooted in the reality that, as Christians, we have been made alive in the Spirit and are children of God. In this lesson, Dr. Godfrey focuses us on our new identities in Christ and the privileges that we have as sons and daughters of God.

LEARNING GOALS

When you have finished this lesson, you should be able to:

- Outline the privileges of being a child of God
- Understand the Spirit's witness and assistance to us in prayer
- Anticipate God's love for you as His child even in the struggle against sin

KEY IDEAS

- In the Christian life, the Spirit gives us life despite the remains of our sinful flesh, and one day, the Spirit will redeem even our bodies.
- In Christ, we are moved from slavery to sonship, enjoy an intimate relationship to God as our Father, and are coheirs with Christ.
- Our relationship to God as Father enables us to cry out to Him through the Spirit in boldness in our struggle against sin, prayer being our great privilege as children.

REFLECTION & DISCUSSION QUESTIONS

Before the Video

What Do You Think?

Take a moment to answer the following questions. They will prepare you for the lecture.

- Why do you eagerly await the redemption of your body?

- What are some of the privileges of being a child of God?

Scripture Reading

Our Father in heaven, hallowed be your name. Your kingdom come, your will be done, on earth as it is in heaven. Give us this day our daily bread, and forgive us our debts, as we also have forgiven our debtors. And lead us not into temptation, but deliver us from evil.

—Matthew 6:9–13

- How did Jesus teach us to address God? In what ways does this relationship make sense to you in regard to the petitions of the Lord's Prayer?

During the Video

Answer the following questions while you watch the video. They will guide you through the lecture.

Alive and Adopted *0:00–7:23*

- What happens if we live according to the flesh and if we live according to the Spirit? What does it mean to live by the Spirit?

- In what sense are we slaves? In what sense are we not slaves?

The Privileges of Sonship *7:23–24:54*

- What does the section of Romans 8 on sonship begin and end with? Why is this significant in our struggle against sin?

- What might Paul's use of an Aramaic term in Romans 8 suggest? What does this term mean?

- How is the need for patience in the Christian life found in this section on adoption in Romans 8?

After the Video

Answer the following questions after you have finished the lecture. They will help you identify and summarize the major points.

- Why is God not characteristically addressed as "Father" in the Old Testament?

  If you are in a group, have the members reflect on whether their privilege of addressing God as Father is something that is taken for granted. Ask: How might we continually remind ourselves of how wonderful a privilege it is to call God "Father"?

- In what ways does the Spirit minister to us as children of God? What do we need to guard ourselves against thinking when we consider the Spirit's ministry for us?

  If you are in a group, have the members read Psalm 38. Ask: Do you typically approach God with the same type of sorrow for sin and yet confidence in prayer? What type of comfort does Romans 8 give you in your struggle against sin?

- How was prayer defined in this lesson? What virtue related to suffering ought to be characteristic of our prayers? What realities should help us to press on?

  If you are in a group, have the members pray the Lord's Prayer out loud, and after praying, ask: How might the theology of Romans 8 shape how you reflect on the petitions of the Lord's Prayer?

PRAYER

Commit what you have learned from God's Word in this lesson to prayer.

- Praise God the Father for His righteousness and for bringing you, though unrighteous, into His family as an adopted child of God.
- Confess any ways that you might take addressing God as your Father for granted, not seeing this privilege in light of who secured it and at what cost.
- Thank God for adopting you as His child and the witness and intercession of the Spirit on your behalf.
- Ask God to help you wait patiently as you suffer, even through your struggle against sin, in the hope of your full redemption in glory.

REVIEW QUIZ

Use these multiple-choice questions to measure what you learned from this lesson.

1. What does the body symbolize in Romans 8?
   a. Death
   b. Life
   c. Pain
   d. Sin

2. Dr. Godfrey argued that the term "son" is intentionally exclusive in Romans 8.
   a. True
   b. False

3. The word *abba* is from what language?
   a. Aramaic
   b. Greek
   c. Hebrew
   d. Latin

4. What psalm may Paul have had in mind when writing Romans 8?
   a. Psalm 16
   b. Psalm 38
   c. Psalm 51
   d. Psalm 103

5. For those in Christ, they are right now children of God.
   a. True
   b. False

6. Which of the following cannot be said of the Christian in light of Romans 8?
   a. We need the intercession of the Spirit.
   b. Our cry to God is a witness of the Spirit about our adoption.
   c. We can be certain that God cares for us in our struggle against sin.
   d. Our expectation in our present life in the body is perfection.

Answer Key—Adopted as Sons

REFLECTION & DISCUSSION QUESTIONS

Before the Video

What Do You Think?

These are personal questions. The answers should be based on your own knowledge and experience.

Scripture Reading

- How did Jesus teach us to address God? In what ways does this relationship make sense to you in regard to the petitions of the Lord's Prayer?

  Jesus taught His disciples to pray, "Our Father . . ." This intimate address to God as our Father is the great privilege that we have through Jesus Christ. The petitions of the Lord's Prayer can be understood in light of this relationship that we enjoy as children to the Father. As children, we desire to see our Father's kingdom and will to be done. As children, we trust our Father to provide for us. As children, we are confident that He will forgive us when we sin, even resembling Him in forgiving others. And as children, we look to Him for protection.

During the Video

Alive and Adopted

- What happens if we live according to the flesh and if we live according to the Spirit? What does it mean to live by the Spirit?

  Paul tells us that those who live according to the flesh will die and that those who live by the Spirit will live (Rom. 8:13). In the context of this teaching, Paul equates life in the Spirit with putting to death the deeds of the body.

- In what sense are we slaves? In what sense are we not slaves?

  As Christians, we can think of ourselves as slaves because we have been made slaves to Jesus Christ and are thus slaves of righteousness (see Rom. 1:1; 6:15–23). We are no longer slaves to sin, and even more than this, we are sons of God. While we can understand our relationship of obedience to the Lord and our God in terms of slavery, our Father relates to us in the most intimate of ways as children.

The Privileges of Sonship

- What does the section of Romans 8 on sonship begin and end with? Why is this significant in our struggle against sin?

  The middle section of Romans 8 deals with the reality of our sonship to God, and this section begins and ends with a focus on prayer. Because Romans 8 is set within the larger section of Romans 6–8, which deals with our struggle over sin to live holy lives, this emphasis on prayer can be understood in relation to that struggle against sin. Even in our struggle against sin, we can cry out to God in prayer, knowing and being encouraged that we are His children.

- What might Paul's use of an Aramaic term in Romans 8 suggest? What does this term mean?

  Paul was writing to the church in Rome, yet he uses an Aramaic term, Abba, *which suggests that the Romans would have been familiar with the term. This further suggests that their familiarity with this term would have come from the liturgy of early Christian worship services.* Abba *is an intimate Aramaic term for "father," and while some believe that "daddy" gets at the sense of the word, Paul does provide us with a definition of the term when he says, "Abba! Father!" (Rom. 8:15).*

- How is the need for patience in the Christian life found in this section on adoption in Romans 8?

  Romans 8:17 particularly stresses our need for patient endurance in the Christian life, since we are "heirs of God and fellow heirs with Christ, provided we suffer with him in order that we may also be glorified with him." As heirs with Christ, we are called to suffer with Him. Before our inheritance, before glory, comes suffering, which requires patient endurance. Even creation groans with longing for redemption and even the full revelation of our sonship (v. 19).

After the Video

- Why is God not characteristically addressed as "Father" in the Old Testament?

  While God was often seen as relating to the nation of Israel and Israel's king as a father, the privilege of addressing God as "Father" is a new covenant reality. The fatherhood of God comes particularly through the sonship of Jesus Christ. It is through faith in Jesus Christ that we have been given the right to become children of God (John 1:12), and it is through Him alone that we have peace with and access to God (Rom. 5:1–2).

- In what ways does the Spirit minister to us as children of God? What do we need to guard ourselves against thinking when we consider the Spirit's ministry for us?

  One of the ways is through His witness bearing that we are indeed children of God. Paul does not mark out a precise answer to how the Spirit bears witness to our spirit that we are children of God. In the context of Romans 8, the Spirit bears witness in the Christian life that He lives in us, giving us strength and encouragement even through our struggle against sin, enabling us to cry out to God in distress. It is in these types of prayers that the Spirit continues to minister to us by interceding for us in our prayers "according to the will of God" (v. 27), even when we do not know what to pray. But although the Spirit ministers to us and on our behalf before the Father, we still ought to pray.

- How was prayer defined in this lesson? What virtue related to suffering ought to be characteristic of our prayers? What realities should help us to press on?

  Prayer was defined as the privilege of intimate communication between the redeemed and their heavenly Father. Prayer is not a mere transmission of information, as though there were things that God did not already know. It is something that we need to see as a privilege and something through which our Father desires our fellowship as we turn to Him and rest in Him. Often in prayer, we may be in distress, and this is why patience is required of us. Paul calls us to endure with Christ in suffering with patience (Rom. 8:16–25), and as Christians, we can endure in patience because of the realities that we presently possess and that await us. We are right now children of God, and the Spirit of God intercedes on our behalf. Along with creation, we await with eagerness the full revelation that we are the children of God on that day when even our bodies will be redeemed.

REVIEW QUIZ

1. **D.**
   Paul speaks about the body in a literal manner in many places, but he may also have in view a symbolic use of the term because of what life in the body entails. Life in the body entails struggle with sin. This reality accompanies life in our bodies now, so we eagerly await the redemption of our bodies, when our struggle with sin will be over.

2. **B.**
   While many may read the language of our being adopted as sons as something that is insensitive to women, in the Greek language and in many other Western languages, the term can be inclusive of both men and women.

3. **A.**
   The word abba, *which Paul uses in Romans 8:15, is Aramaic. Paul defines this word for use immediately, following the word with its equivalent: "Abba! Father!"*

4. **B.**
   Dr. Godfrey focused in on the word "groanings" in Romans 8:26 (see also vv. 22–23) to connect it with Psalm 38, in which David said, "I am feeble and crushed; I groan because of the tumult of my heart" (v. 8).

5. **A.**
   Even though Paul talks about our waiting eagerly for our adoption as sons (Rom. 8:23), it is in relation to the redemption of our bodies. Right now, Christians can know that they are surely sons and daughters of God. Creation itself awaits the revealing of this reality (v. 19), and it is, in fact, a present reality.

6. **D.**
   Perfection is something that we can long for in our present life in the body, but it is not something that we ought to expect. Rather, it is for this very reason that we need the Spirit's intercession and assurance that we are indeed children of God, which gives us full confidence that God cares for us and will not cast us off in our struggle against sin.

14

God's Certain Plan & Good Purpose

INTRODUCTION

As the adopted children of God, Christians enjoy many privileges, and not least of these is the assurance that God is working out a certain plan and good purpose in our lives. Because of how God has already demonstrated His love toward us in Christ, we can trust Him and know that He preserves us in the Christian life. In this lesson, Dr. Godfrey continues outlining the privileges of adoption and enters the final section of Romans 8, which contains some of the most well-known and beloved passages of Scripture.

LEARNING GOALS

When you have finished this lesson, you should be able to:

- Understand the significance of literary features in Romans 8
- Identify why obedience is an important part of the Christian life
- Differentiate between godly and ungodly forms of fear

KEY IDEAS

- Creation itself will one day be set free from its bondage and experience the freedom and glory of the children of God.
- God has a good purpose for us and assures us that all things will work together for good, and we can be assured of this because it is His plan and not our own.
- Predestination is never presented in Scripture as though it were an object of our worry and consternation; it is always an object of encouragement.
- God is for us, so we can know that He lovingly protects and keeps us as Christians.

REFLECTION & DISCUSSION QUESTIONS

Before the Video

What Do You Think?

Take a moment to answer the following questions. They will prepare you for the lecture.

- Why are Christians especially called to exercise patience?

- When is a time that you have questioned what God was doing in your life?

Scripture Reading

For we know that if the tent that is our earthly home is destroyed, we have a building from God, a house not made with hands, eternal in the heavens. For in this tent we groan, longing to put on our heavenly dwelling, if indeed by putting it on we may not be found naked. For while we are still in this tent, we groan, being burdened—not that we would be unclothed, but that we would be further clothed, so that what is mortal may be swallowed up by life. He who has prepared us for this very thing is God, who has given us the Spirit as a guarantee.

—2 Corinthians 5:1–5

- How does this passage connect with passages that you have studied in Romans 7–8?

During the Video

Answer the following questions while you watch the video. They will guide you through the lecture.

Creation's Groaning — *0:00–6:32*

- Why does creation "groan"?

- What is Paul's use of the concept of creation's groaning intended to celebrate?

A Purpose and Plan — *6:32–19:50*

- What does Paul intend the doctrine of predestination to do for the people of God?

- What is the "Golden Chain," and why is this imagery significant?

A Loving Protection *19:50–25:14*

- How can we know that God is for us?

- What are the two accusations of Satan?

After the Video

Answer the following questions after you have finished the lecture. They will help you identify and summarize the major points.

- What ought the knowledge of God's preserving grace to do for us in our process of sanctification? What is an incorrect way of looking at assurance related to sanctification?

  If you are in a group, have the members discuss why assurance of salvation and of God's good purpose and certain plan for us so influences our sanctification and growth in grace.

- What great Old Testament confession of God did Dr. Godfrey highlight? How does it connect to the great promise of Romans 8?

  If you are in a group, have the members read from the following passages and discuss what stands out to them about the contexts in which this great Old Testament confession about God is given: 1 Chronicles 16:1–36; 2 Chronicles 5; Ezra 3.

- "For those whom he foreknew he also predestined to be conformed to the image of his Son" (Rom. 8:29). Why is this verse a comfort to you? Yet what is a way of interpreting this verse that robs you of comfort in the Christian life?

  If you are in a group, have the members share their struggles and moments of insight in coming to embrace the doctrines of grace, particularly the doctrine of predestination or God's unconditional election.

PRAYER

Commit what you have learned from God's Word in this lesson to prayer.

- Praise God as the One who has forever existed as Father, Son, and Holy Spirit.
- Confess any ways that you doubt God's goodness or power or ways that you do not rightly rejoice in them.
- Thank God for sending His precious Son into the world, not sparing His own Son, that we might not be condemned.
- Ask God to help you strive ever more diligently in your sanctification in response to His assurance that He is bringing you all the way through your struggles with sin.

REVIEW QUIZ

Use these multiple-choice questions to measure what you learned from this lesson.

1. What is the center of the chiasm in the third section of Romans 8?
   a. The call to patience
   b. The privilege of prayer
   c. The glory of being a child of God
   d. The redemption of our bodies
2. What image is paired with creation's groanings?
   a. Warfare
   b. Famine
   c. Earthquakes
   d. Birth pangs
3. What doctrine was described by Robert Bellarmine as the chief or principal Protestant heresy?
   a. Adoption
   b. Assurance
   c. Justification
   d. Sanctification
4. What is *not* a part of the "Golden Chain" of Romans 8:30?
   a. Calling
   b. Glorification
   c. Justification
   d. Sanctification
5. The Calvinist interpretation of God's foreknowledge does justice to Paul's purpose in his first mentions of predestination in his letter to the Romans.
   a. True
   b. False

6. What setting provides the language that Paul uses at the end of Romans 8?
    a. Temple
    b. Palace
    c. Courtroom
    d. Church

Answer Key—God's Certain Plan & Good Purpose

REFLECTION & DISCUSSION QUESTIONS

Before the Video

What Do You Think?

These are personal questions. The answers should be based on your own knowledge and experience.

Scripture Reading

- How does this passage connect with passages that you have studied in Romans 7–8?

  Paul's words in 2 Corinthians 5 can be used as an example of how to use Scripture to interpret Scripture. Many of the same themes appear both in this passage and in passages already covered in Romans 7–8. For instance, Paul's cry for deliverance from "this body of death" (7:24) can be connected to the groaning for what is mortal to be "swallowed up by life" (2 Cor. 5:4). The mortal body is a key feature of Romans 8 (see v. 11), which is an expansion of Romans 6:12–14, and the theme of groaning also appears in Romans 8 and 2 Corinthians 5 (see Rom. 8:22–23, 26).

During the Video

Creation's Groaning

- Why does creation "groan"?

  Creation groans because it was subjected to futility, being unable to achieve its created end. Paul compares this groaning to the pains of childbirth. The subjection of creation is described as its "bondage to corruption" (Rom. 8:21).

- What is Paul's use of the concept of creation's groaning intended to celebrate?

  Because of its central place in the chiastic structure of this section of Romans, the idea of creation's groanings and bondage is meant to highlight Paul's main point in this section, and that is the blessedness of the adopted sons and daughters of God. Though we still await the redemption of our bodies, creation longs for what is already ours: "the freedom of the glory of the children of God" (Rom. 8:21).

A Purpose and Plan

- What does Paul intend the doctrine of predestination to do for the people of God?

  When Paul introduces the doctrine of predestination, which he does for the first time in his letter in the fourth section of Romans 8, it is intended to encourage God's people. Predestination is not an object of our worry, and though it can be a doctrine that people wrestle with, it is a doctrine of comfort and encouragement in the Christian life that fits perfectly with the wonderful promises of assurance in Romans 8.

- What is the "Golden Chain," and why is this imagery significant?

  What Reformed theologians have called the "Golden Chain" is found in Romans 8:30: "And those whom he predestined he also called, and those whom he called he also justified, and those whom he justified he also glorified." The imagery of a chain linking all these acts of God's grace communicates to us that God has enacted a certain plan in our salvation, that our predestination in Christ in eternity past is certainly worked out in history in our calling and justification, and in the future in our glorification.

A Loving Protection

- How can we know that God is for us?

  Romans 8 ends with a string of assurances that God is for us, and if God is for us, then nothing can be against us. Paul assures us that God is for us by pointing to what God has already done for us in Christ: "He who did not spare his own Son but gave him up for us all, how will he not also with him graciously give us all things?" (v. 32).

- What are the two accusations of Satan?

  Satan has two standard accusations. First, he accuses God, saying to us, "You cannot trust God," which is not true. Second, he accuses us before God, saying, "They are sinners," which is a true accusation but not one that we should fear because God justifies His elect in Christ alone, who has already faced condemnation on our behalf.

After the Video

- What ought the knowledge of God's preserving grace to do for us in our process of sanctification? What is an incorrect way of looking at assurance related to sanctification?

  The knowledge that God preserves and protects us in the Christian life ought to lead us into greater efforts to be holy as God is holy. Rather than leading us to laziness and indifference in the Christian life, assurance of salvation ought to lead us to strive all the more in our sanctification. It changes everything to know that we will have certain victory over sin because it is God's will for us, and this should encourage us in our struggle against sin.

- What great Old Testament confession of God did Dr. Godfrey highlight? How does it connect to the great promise of Romans 8?

  The great Old Testament confession that Dr. Godfrey highlighted and is used throughout the Psalms is "Give thanks to the LORD, for he is good, for his steadfast love endures forever!" (see Pss. 106:1; 107:1; 118:29; 136:1ff.). This great confession connects to the renowned promises of Romans 8, "And we know that for those who love God all things work together for good, for those who are called according to his purpose" (v. 28). God works out all things for our good because it is His nature to do so for those who love Him, for His love endures forever. This is an especially important reminder in our struggles because it can be tempting to doubt God's goodness, though it ought to be our source of great comfort.

- "For those whom he foreknew he also predestined to be conformed to the image of his Son" (Rom. 8:29). Why is this verse a comfort to you? Yet what is a way of interpreting this verse that robs you of comfort in the Christian life?

  This verse is a great comfort to Christians because it assures us that God has predestined us to be like His Son such that we are being preserved even through our struggles against sin. If we interpret the concept of foreknowledge incorrectly, however, this passage does not provide any comfort at all. Romans 8:29 does not mean that God foresees how we will respond to His grace and thus He predestines our salvation and conformity to Christ in reaction to our response. This would place our salvation and sanctification in our own hands. If we understand that Paul is attempting to provide encouragement to Christians in this passage, assuring us that our salvation is God's sovereign plan, then we can guard ourselves against such an interpretation.

REVIEW QUIZ

1. **C.**

   Romans 8:20–21 forms part of the central portion of this chiasm, and it reads, "For the creation was subjected to futility, not willingly, but because of him who subjected it, in hope that the creation itself will be set free from its bondage to corruption and obtain the freedom of the glory of the children of God." Paul wants us to rejoice in the freedom that we already have as children of God, and the literary structure of this passage highlights this.

2. **D.**

   The image that is paired to creation's groanings is fitting for a passage that deals with the revelation of the children of God. Paul says, "For we know that the whole creation has been groaning together in the pains of childbirth until now" (Rom. 8:22).

3. **B.**

   Though one might expect that the Protestant doctrine of justification by faith alone would incur such a strong reaction, the Roman Catholic theologian Robert Bellarmine said that the doctrine of assurance is the chief or principal Protestant heresy.

4. **D.**
   Though Paul mentions our being predestined for conformity to Christ in Romans 8:29, he does not mention anything like sanctification in the "Golden Chain" of Romans 8:30. Dr. Godfrey stressed that Paul, in leaving sanctification out of this list, teaches us that our sanctification is not determinative of our salvation—God is.

5. **A.**
   If foreknowledge is understood as God's looking down the corridors of time to see whether we would believe and predestining us in response to our foreseen faith, then Paul's purpose of introducing predestination as a comfort to Christians would be lost. A Calvinist understanding of foreknowledge as God's certain plan does justice to Paul's intent.

6. **C.**
   The list of questions in Romans 8:31–35, particularly verses 33–34, brings to mind a law court; Paul uses language such as "charge," "justifies," and "condemn." Christ's death, resurrection, ascension, and intercession for us at the right hand of the Father assure us that we cannot be condemned.

15

God's Loving Protection

INTRODUCTION

Romans 8, though ending a major section in Paul's letter, logically flows into Romans 9. Paul drives home the rich security we have in Christ in Romans 8, but he then needs to address a question that may loom larger in the mind of his readers: But what about Israel? In this lesson, Dr. Godfrey connects Romans 8 to Romans 9, showing the thematic unity between these chapters and transitioning into Paul's next line of argument that runs through Romans 9–11.

LEARNING GOALS

When you have finished this lesson, you should be able to:

- Answer how Romans 8 helps us to process our suffering for righteousness' sake
- Understand Paul's use of the Old Testament in Romans 8–9
- Describe the connection between Romans 8–9 and features of the literary structure of Romans 9–11

KEY IDEAS

- Nothing in creation can separate us from the love of Christ.
- We must see our suffering as fulfilling God's purpose, which means not that we must embrace our suffering but that we must cry out to Him all the more through patient prayers for deliverance.
- God's loving protection of His people in Romans 8 and the question of Israel in Romans 9 are directly connected, for God's Word does not fail concerning His people.

REFLECTION & DISCUSSION QUESTIONS

Before the Video

What Do You Think?

Take a moment to answer the following questions. They will prepare you for the lecture.

- Have you ever endured suffering for righteousness' sake? How did you cope with it?

- Why would Paul need to explain, as it relates to Israel, what was happening in history as the gospel went forth to the nations?

Scripture Reading

Behold, the hour is coming, indeed it has come, when you will be scattered, each to his own home, and will leave me alone. Yet I am not alone, for the Father is with me. I have said these things to you, that in me you may have peace. In the world you will have tribulation. But take heart; I have overcome the world.

—John 16:32–33

The band of soldiers and their captain and the officers of the Jews arrested Jesus and bound him.

—John 18:12

- What seems to be at odds in these two passages?

During the Video

Answer the following questions while you watch the video. They will guide you through the lecture.

Righteous Suffering *0:00–12:10*

- What is implied in Paul's list of dangers after asking, "Who shall separate us from the love of Christ?" (Rom. 8:35)?

- What is unique about the suffering described in Psalm 44?

- How is Psalm 45 relevant to the theology of Romans 8?

The Bridge between Romans 8 and 9 *12:10–24:37*

- Why does Paul address the problem of Israel after Romans 8?

- What features suggest that Romans 9–11 can be understood as a chiasm?

After the Video

Answer the following questions after you have finished the lecture. They will help you identify and summarize the major points.

- Reflecting on the end of Romans 8, how ought we to suffer as Christians?

  If you are in a group, have the members read Psalms 44–45. Ask: What particularly about these psalms encourages you?

- Why is Paul so vexed about Israel? What is he so careful to be clear about when it comes to God's relationship with Israel?

  If you are in a group, have the members read Romans 9:1–3 and discuss how Paul's vexation for Israel ought to inform the Christian's heart for the lost.

- What is "true Israel"? How does Paul begin to prove out the theology behind this idea in Romans 9? Why does Paul make such a distinction within Israel?

  If you are in a group, have the members discuss why the idea of a true Israel is resonant even today in an evangelical context.

PRAYER

Commit what you have learned from God's Word in this lesson to prayer.

- Praise God for His power to preserve you through anything that would threaten to separate you from the love of Christ.
- Confess ways that you have lost patience with God and have lost sight of the fact that He is working out His purposes in your life.
- Thank God that He has been faithful to His people throughout history.
- Ask God to prepare your heart to marvel at His electing grace as you study Romans 9.

REVIEW QUIZ

Use these multiple-choice questions to measure what you learned from this lesson.

1. What is Paul's great and primary point at the end of Romans 8?
   a. God has an eternal plan and purpose for us.
   b. Nothing can separate us from the love of Christ.
   c. Our suffering as Christians is not meaningless.
   d. Sonship is the blessed reality of believers.
2. What psalm does Paul quote from at the end of Romans 8?
   a. Psalm 1
   b. Psalm 19
   c. Psalm 44
   d. Psalm 51
3. Romans 8 teaches us to maintain a stoic mindset in our suffering.
   a. True
   b. False
4. What is *not* one of the great blessings that Paul lists as belonging to Israel?
   a. Adoption
   b. Covenants
   c. Creation
   d. Patriarchs
5. Romans 8 has more quotations from the Old Testament than Romans 9.
   a. True
   b. False
6. What is *not* one of the three topics that people often think about relating to each of the chapters in Romans 9–11?
   a. Israel's future
   b. Predestination
   c. Sanctification
   d. The importance of preaching

Answer Key—God's Loving Protection

REFLECTION & DISCUSSION QUESTIONS

Before the Video

What Do You Think?

These are personal questions. The answers should be based on your own knowledge and experience.

Scripture Reading

- What seems to be at odds in these two passages?

  In John 16, Jesus assures His disciples in the face of what was to come and the tribulation that they would experience in the world. The ground of His assurance is that He has "overcome the world," yet shortly after Jesus said these words, He was betrayed, arrested, and crucified. Even while Jesus appeared to be at His most helpless, He was more than a conqueror, and this ought to give us confidence that we, too, are more than conquerors in Christ, even amid our suffering.

During the Video

Righteous Suffering

- What is implied in Paul's list of dangers after asking, "Who shall separate us from the love of Christ?" (Rom. 8:35)?

  Paul follows this question in the same verse with another one: "Shall tribulation, or distress, or persecution, or famine, or nakedness, or danger, or sword?" By naming these things, the Apostle implies that though nothing can separate us from the love of Christ, these are things that we may have to face and be brought through as Christians.

- What is unique about the suffering described in Psalm 44?

  Many times in the Psalms, God's people cry out to Him about their suffering, and many times, they own up to the fact that their suffering is on account of their sin. Psalm 44, however, is full of confidence in the faithfulness of God's people, which causes great dismay over their suffering. Paul quotes Psalm 44 to underscore that God's people do suffer for His sake and that He is nonetheless faithful to save.

- How is Psalm 45 relevant to the theology of Romans 8?

  Though Paul does not quote Psalm 45 in Romans 8, he does quote Psalm 44, which leads to some rich theological reflection about the relationship between these two psalms and Romans 8. Psalm 44 is a cry to God on account of righteous suffering, and Psalm 45 is a great celebration of the King who will deliver Israel, which closely aligns with the assurance of victory in Romans 8.

The Bridge between Romans 8 and 9

- Why does Paul address the problem of Israel after Romans 8?

  Throughout Romans 8, Paul had been extolling God's loving protection of His people, but questions may arise in the minds of many: What about Israel? Aren't the promises in Romans 8 the same types of promises that God made to Israel? How can Christians be truly assured of these promises? Paul needs to address these potential questions as well as the criticisms that he may be facing relating to his understanding of Israel and interpretation of the Old Testament.

- What features suggest that Romans 9–11 can be understood as a chiasm?

  The chiastic nature of Romans 9–11 will be elaborated on more fully, but the initial hint that this section of Romans can be understood this way is the section's beginning and ending. This section begins in Romans 9 with Paul's emotional distress over Israel, and it ends in Romans 11 with his joyful response to God's working out of salvation through history. Both the beginning of Romans 9 and the end of Romans 11 contain a doxology that ends with "Amen" (9:5; 11:36).

After the Video

- Reflecting on the end of Romans 8, how ought we to suffer as Christians?

  Romans 8 is not a call for us to love and embrace our suffering or even to be stoic about our suffering. In a real sense, Romans 8 helps us to respond appropriately to suffering. In our suffering, we can cry out to God as our Father, trusting that He has a purpose in our suffering, which enables us to be patient through it even while we pray to be delivered from it.

- Why is Paul so vexed about Israel? What is he so careful to be clear about when it comes to God's relationship with Israel?

  Paul is vexed about Israel for many reasons. Not only is Paul concerned with defending God's righteousness, he longs for the salvation of his kinsmen. What makes Paul's vexation all the more great is the manifold blessings that the people of Israel had experienced: "They are Israelites, and to them belong the adoption, the glory, the covenants, the giving of the law, the worship, and the promises. To them belong the patriarchs, and from their race, according to the flesh, is the Christ" (Rom. 9:4–5). Despite the apparent unresponsiveness of Israel to the gospel, Paul is emphatic that God's Word has not failed concerning Israel.

- What is "true Israel"? How does Paul begin to prove out the theology behind this idea in Romans 9? Why does Paul make such a distinction within Israel?

  In Romans 9:6, Paul says, "Not all who are descended from Israel belong to Israel." The idea of a true Israel is connected to this and distinguishes between a merely physical Israel and a spiritual Israel. Paul introduces this idea to show that the Word of God has not failed with Israel, and this can be seen throughout Israel's history. Paul traces this idea of a physical and a spiritual Israel all the way back to

Abraham, distinguishing between Ishmael and Isaac, as well as Isaac's children, Esau and Jacob.

REVIEW QUIZ

1. **B.**
   Though some of these themes occur in Romans 8 and are significant, Paul's great point at the end of the chapter is that nothing can separate us from the love of Christ (v. 35). Romans 8 begins with the declaration that there is no condemnation in Jesus Christ and ends with the promise that nothing can separate us from this love of God in Christ.

2. **C.**
   Psalm 44 is perhaps less well known than Psalms 1, 19, and 51, but Paul quotes from it at the end of Romans 8 to help Christians understand that even through our faithful suffering, God is for us. Even if we are being persecuted for His sake, nothing can separate us from His love.

3. **B.**
   Romans 8 helps us understand that our suffering does not sever us from the love of God in Jesus Christ and that our suffering fulfills His purposes. To be stoic about our suffering would mean that we would not react to it as if it were suffering but would rather remain unaffected by it. The cry for deliverance "Abba! Father!" earlier in Romans 8 teaches us that we ought to cry out to God in our suffering.

4. **C.**
   At the heart of Paul's lament for his kinsmen is that great gifts had been given to Israel: "They are Israelites, and to them belong the adoption, the glory, the covenants, the giving of the law, the worship, and the promises. To them belong the patriarchs, and from their race, according to the flesh, is the Christ, who is God over all, blessed forever" (Rom. 9:4–5). Creation is a broader category than these gifts, which are significant in the history of redemption.

5. **B.**
   There is only one quotation from the Old Testament in Romans 8, whereas in Romans 9, Paul quotes the Old Testament more than thirty times to vindicate his reading of the Old Testament and what he understands to be God's work and plan for Israel.

6. **C.**
   Sanctification is the significant theme in Romans 6–8. When it comes to Romans 9–11, people often divide the chapters into topics rather than seeing them as a whole, believing then that Romans 9 deals only with predestination, with Romans 10 highlighting the primacy of preaching and Romans 11 the future of Israel.

16

Israel & God's Purpose

INTRODUCTION

Paul was in anguish about his fellow Israelites who had and were rejecting Jesus Christ, and he needed to give an answer that God had not forsaken His covenant people. God's Word had not failed but was being fulfilled. In this lesson, Dr. Godfrey shows how Romans 9–11 forms a chiasm that explains how God's purpose with Israel and the ingrafting of the gentiles was all according to plan and was the same message that God had been giving His people about the necessity of faith and humble reliance on His Word.

LEARNING GOALS

When you have finished this lesson, you should be able to:

- Understand the doctrine of election in the context of Romans 9–11
- Explain Paul's use of the Old Testament to explain his historical moment
- Identify how Paul demonstrates the necessity of the faith as opposed to a works-righteousness in the old covenant

KEY IDEAS

- At the point in history in which Paul was writing, God was doing with Israel and the other nations what He had always said He would do.
- God elects and is long-suffering in His judgment because of His great mercy.
- Israel had misinterpreted the purpose of the law of Moses, believing that righteousness could be earned from it.

REFLECTION & DISCUSSION QUESTIONS

Before the Video

What Do You Think?

Take a moment to answer the following questions. They will prepare you for the lecture.

- Do you struggle or have you struggled to embrace the doctrine of election?

- What attributes of God come to mind when you reflect on the doctrine of election?

Scripture Reading

In that day the remnant of Israel and the survivors of the house of Jacob will no more lean on him who struck them, but will lean on the LORD, the Holy One of Israel, in truth. A remnant will return, the remnant of Jacob, to the mighty God. For though your people Israel be as the sand of the sea, only a remnant of them will return. Destruction is decreed, overflowing with righteousness. For the Lord GOD of hosts will make a full end, as decreed, in the midst of all the earth.

—Isaiah 10:20–23

- Considering what was going on with Israel when Paul was writing, how is this passage fulfilled? How is it also filled with hope for Israel?

During the Video

Answer the following questions while you watch the video. They will guide you through the lecture.

Paul's Purposes *0:00–6:12*

- What very particular thing is Paul focused on in his expansive discussion of God's relationship with Israel and purpose in history?

- Why does Paul quote the Old Testament so frequently in Romans 9–11?

- What does Paul mean in quoting from Malachi about Esau and Jacob? What doesn't he mean?

Paul's Responses *6:12–12:20*

- What are some of the questions that Paul imagines being asked and that he responds to in Romans 9?

- What question does Paul ask in response to the people who he knows will ask these types of questions?

God's Purposes *12:20–25:17*

- What does Paul reveal about God's plans in quoting from Hosea and Isaiah in Romans 9:25–29?

- Why had Israel failed?

After the Video

Answer the following questions after you have finished the lecture. They will help you identify and summarize the major points.

- When people think of election, God's sovereignty in salvation typically comes to mind. God is sovereign, but Paul also stresses another attribute of God when talking about election. What is it, and how should it inform the way that we talk about election?

  If you are in a group, have the members share any encounters that they may have had with people who have bristled at the idea of election. Ask: What sort of tack ought we to take when talking with people about such a difficult subject for them?

- In your estimation, why are Romans 9 and 10 incredibly humbling chapters of the Bible?

  If you are in a group, have the members describe their first encounters with Romans 9. Ask: Is the doctrine of election something that you have ever struggled to embrace?

- How is it that Paul is not contradicting himself when he quotes Moses, who said, "The person who does the commandments shall live by them" (Rom. 10:5)?

If you are in a group, have the members discuss and review Romans 9–10 to draw out how the necessity of faith and the necessity of the Word of God are seen in these chapters.

PRAYER

Commit what you have learned from God's Word in this lesson to prayer.

- Praise God for His gracious character and your election in Christ.
- Confess ways that you lose sight of God's great mercy and fail in giving thanks as you ought.
- Thank God for His making a way in Christ for righteousness through faith.
- Ask God to help you see His grace particularly in studying the difficult questions related to God's old covenant people over the course of this study and those to come.

REVIEW QUIZ

Use these multiple-choice questions to measure what you learned from this lesson.

1. What is *not* one of the key words of the chiasm of Romans 9–11?
   a. Paul
   b. Israel
   c. Faith
   d. Sin
2. Why are Esau and Jacob, in Paul's argument, excellent examples of God's purpose in election?
   a. Esau sold his birthright to Jacob.
   b. Jacob was deceptive and no better than Esau.
   c. Esau—but not Jacob—took for himself a foreign wife.
   d. Jacob and Esau were twins, yet the birthright was not according to works or birth order.
3. "The person who does the commandments shall live by them" (Rom. 10:5; see also Lev. 18:5) must be interpreted in terms of a righteousness that is attainable by works.
   a. True
   b. False
4. What attribute of God is Paul highlighting in relation to election in Romans 9?
   a. Aseity
   b. Holiness
   c. Mercy
   d. Omniscience

5. How is fallen humanity depicted in Romans 9?
   a. As Esau
   b. As Pharaoh
   c. As a potter
   d. As clay
6. What minor prophet does Paul quote to support God's plan for the gentiles in the Old Testament?
   a. Amos
   b. Hosea
   c. Joel
   d. Malachi

Answer Key—Israel & God's Purpose

REFLECTION & DISCUSSION QUESTIONS

Before the Video

What Do You Think?

These are personal questions. The answers should be based on your own knowledge and experience.

Scripture Reading

- Considering what was going on with Israel when Paul was writing, how is this passage fulfilled? How is it also filled with hope for Israel?

  Paul was in agony for his fellow Israelites. They had rejected the Messiah. In this sense, destruction had come upon Israel. Paul calls this a "partial hardening" in Romans 11:25. Yet there was still hope for Israel, for God was saving a remnant from Israel as He had done in times past. Paul himself was evidence of God's saving work (see Rom. 11:1).

During the Video

Paul's Purposes

- What very particular thing is Paul focused on in his expansive discussion of God's relationship with Israel and purpose in history?

  Romans 11 deals with Israel and God's covenant and purpose in history. Yet Paul does not say everything there is to say about these expansive topics. He has something very particular in mind: to show that God's Word to Israel had not failed.

- Why does Paul quote the Old Testament so frequently in Romans 9–11?

  The major question that Paul is answering is "Has God's Word failed?" (see Rom. 9:6). Throughout Romans 9–11, Paul is showing how God's promises, far from being called into question, are actually being fulfilled. His copious quotation of the Old Testament demonstrates this. Paul's teaching about what God was doing with Israel and the gentiles was not something that he had invented but something that had been prophesied.

- What does Paul mean in quoting from Malachi about Esau and Jacob? What doesn't he mean?

  Paul quotes Malachi about Esau and Jacob to support his teaching about God's election as something that is not based on works. God showed favor to Jacob even before he was born and even though he was not the firstborn as was Esau. Many call the doctrine of election into question in Romans 9 by appealing to Paul's quotation of Malachi, believing that it refers to nations only and not individuals, but the reason why God loved Israel over Edom (Esau's descendants) is that He first loved or elected the individual Jacob and hated Esau.

Paul's Responses

- What are some of the questions that Paul imagines being asked and that he responds to in Romans 9?

  Paul anticipates a number of questions based on his teaching about election in Romans 9. If God elects without reference to works: "What shall we say then? Is there injustice on God's part?" (v. 14). Also, if God elects without reference to works: "Why does he still find fault? For who can resist his will?" (v. 19).

- What question does Paul ask in response to the people who he knows will ask these types of questions?

  In response to those who would raise these types of issues, which question God's character, Paul says, "Who are you, O man, to answer back to God?" (Rom. 9:20), reminding us that we are mere creatures who dare not answer back to the Creator. Paul likens this relationship to one between a potter and clay.

God's Purposes

- What does Paul reveal about God's plans in quoting from Hosea and Isaiah in Romans 9:25–29?

  Paul quotes Hosea 1:10 and 2:23 to show how God had planned to save the gentiles. In God's plan, the gentiles would become His "vessels of mercy" (Rom. 9:23–24). In quoting from Isaiah 10:22–23, Paul likewise shows how Israel's judgment was long foretold, yet also that God was saving a remnant for Himself.

- Why had Israel failed?

  The people of Israel had failed, though they had been given the law, because they pursued the law as if it were something through which they could attain righteousness. The law was not given to drive Israel to a works-righteousness. It was to be pursued by faith and not by works.

After the Video

- When people think of election, God's sovereignty in salvation typically comes to mind. God is sovereign, but Paul also stresses another attribute of God when talking about election. What is it, and how should it inform the way that we talk about election?

  When Paul teaches about election in Romans 9, it is not merely to exalt the sovereignty of God in salvation but also to extol God's mercy. Instead of asking, "Why doesn't God save everyone?," we should ask, "Why does God save anyone?" God is not under any obligation to have mercy on anyone; we cannot claim a right to

His mercy. Yet God does have mercy and compassion on whomever He wills. We should be surprised and overwhelmed by God's mercy and love to us in election. God's electing love should never lead us to question His character or to complain.

- In your estimation, why are Romans 9 and 10 incredibly humbling chapters of the Bible?

  Answers to this question may vary and to varying degrees be personal in nature but should consider key themes of Romans 9, including but not limited to election, God's sovereignty, and the necessity of faith for salvation.

- How is it that Paul is not contradicting himself when he quotes Moses, who said, "The person who does the commandments shall live by them" (Rom. 10:5)?

  In Romans 9, Paul speaks about Israel's failure in pursuing a law that would lead to righteousness (v. 31), and in Romans 10, he speaks about "the righteousness that is based on the law" (v. 5). It seems here that Paul speaks of the law as something that could be used to attain righteousness, but earlier he said that Israel had failed in its approach to the law "as if it were based on works" (9:32). Paul is not contradicting himself but is still showing how Israel fundamentally misunderstood the purpose of the law, the right understanding of which can be found even in Moses. By next quoting from Deuteronomy 30:12–14, Paul demonstrates that even the Mosaic covenant was gracious and that Moses was calling Israel to faith in the mercies of God.

REVIEW QUIZ

1. **D.**
   Though sin *is an instrumental part of Israel's failure and the necessity of God's merciful election and gift of faith, it was not one of the words that Dr. Godfrey used to describe the chiastic literary structure of Romans 9–11, which were* Paul, Israel, God's purpose, faith, *and* Word.

2. **D.**
   While some of these facts could be appealed to as reasons to see God's election shine through in the lives of Jacob and Esau, Paul uses them as perfect examples of God's purpose of election in that they were twins, and that before they were out of the womb to do anything and even despite their birth order, God's electing grace was already upon Jacob and not Esau.

3. **B.**
   When this statement is taken by itself, it would be easier to interpret it in the way that Israel had interpreted it. But when it is taken together with other statements of Moses, such as Deuteronomy 30:12–14, which Paul also quoted in Romans 10, we can understand that the law was never given so that God's people could attain righteousness by works.

4. **C.**
Each of God's attributes can be related to election in some way, but Paul is highlighting God's mercy in Romans 9, for as God says, "I will have mercy on whom I have mercy, and I will have compassion on whom I have compassion" (v. 15; see also Ex. 33:19).

5. **D.**
Paul uses the illustration of a potter's relationship to the clay that he forms to communicate our relationship to God in His electing purposes. He is the Creator and we are His creatures, part of the fallen lump of humanity, who need His sovereign mercy for salvation.

6. **B.**
In Romans 9, Paul quotes from Isaiah to explain how Israel's judgment was foretold by God in the Old Testament, and he quotes from the minor prophet Hosea to explain how God's plan for the gentiles was also long established.

17

The Central Promise of Salvation

INTRODUCTION

Romans 9–11 is filled with theologically rich themes, such as election and the salvation of Israel, and these often introduce perplexing questions. The complexity of Paul's thought in these chapters can be simplified if we understand his main point. In this lesson, Dr. Godfrey takes us to the center of the chiasm of Romans 9–11, to the great promise of salvation that is given to all—Jews and gentiles alike—who call on the name of the Lord.

LEARNING GOALS

When you have finished this lesson, you should be able to:

- Identify the central message of Romans 9–11 and how it applies to the themes of these chapters and our lives
- Explain why preaching is vital for working out God's plan of salvation
- Understand Paul's teaching about what God was and is doing with His old covenant people

KEY IDEAS

- The heart of the chiasm in Romans 9–11 is a great promise of salvation that helps to focus our questions about election, God's justice, and Israel on a central, simple message.
- Preaching is not only how people hear about Jesus but also how they hear Jesus.
- Just as God was saving the nations in Paul's day, He was also saving Israelites and continues to do so today.

REFLECTION & DISCUSSION QUESTIONS

Before the Video

What Do You Think?

Take a moment to answer the following questions. They will prepare you for the lecture.

- What is difficult about evangelism for you?

- How has preaching been instrumental in your faith and why?

Scripture Reading

And I will show wonders in the heavens and on the earth, blood and fire and columns of smoke. The sun shall be turned to darkness, and the moon to blood, before the great and awesome day of the LORD comes. And it shall come to pass that everyone who calls on the name of the LORD shall be saved. For in Mount Zion and in Jerusalem there shall be those who escape, as the LORD has said, and among the survivors shall be those whom the LORD calls.

—Joel 2:30–32

- How does this passage illustrate that God is sovereign in salvation and yet that we also have a responsibility to believe?

During the Video

Answer the following questions while you watch the video. They will guide you through the lecture.

The Heart of Romans 9–11 *0:00–11:01*

- What is the heart of the chiasm of Romans 9–11? How is this passage applied in Acts 2? How does this fit the context of this passage in Romans?

- Why is Jesus' statement "Not everyone who says to me, 'Lord, Lord,' will enter the kingdom of heaven" (Matt. 7:21) not a contradiction of this central message?

God's Word and Israel *11:01–24:11*

- What difference of translation does Dr. Godfrey take for Romans 10:14? What can this teach us about the nature of preaching?

- What is God's purpose for Israel in saving the nations? What is Paul's basic answer to the question "What is God doing with Israel?"

After the Video

Answer the following questions after you have finished the lecture. They will help you identify and summarize the major points.

- In what two ways did Dr. Godfrey apply the central promise of Romans 9–11 to our reading of these chapters and our lives more broadly? Which of these is more helpful to you and why?

  If you are in a group, have the members discuss their questions and struggles relevant to the two major points of application that Dr. Godfrey made.

- How can the deity of Christ be proved from Paul's quotation of the Old Testament at the center of Romans 9–11 and Peter's use of the same passage in Acts 2?

  If you are in a group, have the members read Acts 2 for the full context of Peter's quotation. Ask: What does this chapter reveal about Jesus and the type of life that He brings about?

- What well-known story from the Old Testament does Paul make use of at the beginning of Romans 11? What is his point, and what implications of this passage might you draw for people today?

  If you are in a group, have the members read 1 Kings 19:9–18 and compare this passage to Romans 9:1–3. Ask: What is different about Paul's take on Israel? How might Paul have been informed by this other account?

PRAYER

Commit what you have learned from God's Word in this lesson to prayer.

- Praise God for His sovereign work in bringing people to a place to call on Him.

- Confess ways that you doubt (perhaps not even consciously) God's ability or willingness to save those who might appear to be far off—family, friends, or different groups of people.
- Thank God for His certain promise that all who call on His name will be saved.
- Ask God to give you the patience not to despair in His working for those whom you long to see come to faith in Jesus Christ and to give you the persistence in continuing to tell others about Him.

REVIEW QUIZ

Use these multiple-choice questions to measure what you learned from this lesson.

1. What book of the Bible is Paul quoting from at the heart of Romans 9–11?
   a. Exodus
   b. Leviticus
   c. Isaiah
   d. Joel
2. One merely has to make a public confession that Jesus is Lord to be saved.
   a. True
   b. False
3. What is *not* one of the things that Dr. Godfrey connected the central promise of Romans 9–11 to?
   a. The day of the Lord
   b. The deity of Jesus Christ
   c. Encouragement in evangelism
   d. Worrying about election
4. A valid way of translating Romans 10:14 communicates that when we hear the preached Word, we hear Christ.
   a. True
   b. False
5. What does Paul stress about God's work among the Israelites?
   a. God is finally finished with His old covenant people.
   b. God is right now saving some from among Israel.
   c. God is still planning for Israel's future salvation.
   d. God is disproportionately saving Israelites.
6. What person from the Old Testament does Paul bring up in connection to God's work in Israel?
   a. Abraham
   b. Adam
   c. David
   d. Elijah

Answer Key—The Central Promise of Salvation

REFLECTION & DISCUSSION QUESTIONS

Before the Video

What Do You Think?

These are personal questions. The answers should be based on your own knowledge and experience.

Scripture Reading

- How does this passage illustrate that God is sovereign in salvation and yet that we also have a responsibility to believe?

  The great promise of this passage is "Everyone who calls on the name of the LORD shall be saved." We are called to call on the name of the Lord for salvation. Yet God is also at work sovereignly in all who answer this call, for those who are saved are "those whom the LORD calls."

During the Video

The Heart of Romans 9–11

- What is the heart of the chiasm of Romans 9–11? How is this passage applied in Acts 2? How does this fit the context of this passage in Romans?

  The heart of the chiasm of Romans 9–11 is "For 'everyone who calls on the name of the Lord will be saved'" (10:13). Paul quotes this passage from Joel 2:32, which Peter also quotes when preaching on the day of Pentecost. On that day, in fulfillment of Joel's prophecy, God's Spirit was poured out on all flesh. In this section of Romans, Paul is also dealing with topics related to Israel and the nations. The preceding verses read: "For the Scripture says, 'Everyone who believes in him will not be put to shame.' For there is no distinction between Jew and Greek; for the same Lord is Lord of all, bestowing his riches on all who call on him" (10:11–12).

- Why is Jesus' statement "Not everyone who says to me, 'Lord, Lord,' will enter the kingdom of heaven" (Matt. 7:21) not a contradiction of this central message?

  God promises that everyone who calls on Him will be saved, yet in the Sermon on the Mount, Jesus said, "Not everyone who says to me, 'Lord, Lord,' will enter the kingdom of heaven" (7:21). Understanding both the passage in Romans and the one in the Sermon on the Mount passage in context is key. Paul previously spoke about confession that is from the heart (Rom. 10:9–10), and such a heartfelt confession is not what Jesus had in mind when He spoke these words in the Sermon on the Mount. We have to be sincere in our confession of the Lord, and according to Jesus, such sincerity will manifest itself in doing God's will.

God's Word and Israel

- What difference of translation does Dr. Godfrey take for Romans 10:14? What can this teach us about the nature of preaching?

  Romans 10:14, in the English Standard Version, reads: "And how are they to believe in him of whom they have never heard?" Another way of translating this verse would be to render the phrase "of whom" as "whom." What this means for how we understand the nature of preaching is that it's not fundamentally a preacher telling us about Christ; it is actually Christ Himself speaking to us in the ministry of His Word.

- What is God's purpose for Israel in saving the nations? What is Paul's basic answer to the question "What is God doing with Israel?"

  God's purpose with Israel is to make His old covenant people jealous through His work among the nations. This work of God was going on in Paul's day, so his basic answer to the question about what God was doing with Israel is that He is right now saving some from among Israel, the remnant of His people.

After the Video

- In what two ways did Dr. Godfrey apply the central promise of Romans 9–11 to our reading of these chapters and our lives more broadly? Which of these is more helpful to you and why?

  The two areas of practical application that were developed from the central promise of Romans 9–11 are how this great promise helps us relate to the doctrines in Romans 9–11 and how this great promise helps us to be faithful in our evangelism. Related to the first area, the fact that Paul is making a central point that all who call on the Lord will be saved puts the doctrine of election and questions about Israel in context. Personally, this promise can free us from worry about our individual election because we can rest in the promises that God will save all who call on Him. Related to the second area, this promise can bring us to greater faithfulness in evangelism because telling someone that God will save all who call on Him carries with it a call to action: Call on Him!

- How can the deity of Christ be proved from Paul's quotation of the Old Testament at the center of Romans 9–11 and Peter's use of the same passage in Acts 2?

  Joel 2 uses the divine name when God promised that "everyone who calls on the name of the Lord shall be saved" (v. 32). When Paul quotes this verse in Romans 10, Jesus Christ is in view, for the Apostle says that "if you confess with your mouth that Jesus is Lord and believe in your heart that God raised him from the dead, you will be saved" (v. 9). Likewise, in Acts 2, Peter calls people to faith in Christ after quoting from Joel 2 (see Acts 2:14–41). These connections demonstrate that the man Jesus Christ is God.

- What well-known story from the Old Testament does Paul make use of at the beginning of Romans 11? What is his point, and what implications of this passage might you draw for people today?

  Elijah was a faithful prophet of the Lord, but he despaired over the apostasy in Israel. Paul quotes from 1 Kings 19, when Elijah fled to a cave, giving up hope on Israel and bringing charges to God against Israel. God responded to Elijah's belief that he alone was left faithful among Israel by declaring that "I will leave seven thousand in Israel, all the knees that have not bowed to Baal" (v. 18). God was saving a remnant for Himself from Israel, as He is doing now. The answer to the last question requires you to connect Paul's thought about Israel to today. One possible implication that may be drawn from this episode in Elijah's life in relation to Paul's teaching in Romans is that we ought not to despair when we do not see fruit in our evangelism; like Elijah, we might not always know how God is working.

REVIEW QUIZ

1. **D.**

   At the heart of Romans 9–11, Paul quotes from the book of Joel: "And it shall come to pass that everyone who calls on the name of the Lord *shall be saved" (2:32). This is Paul's central message in these chapters.*

2. **B.**

   Romans 10 teaches us that "with the heart one believes and is justified, and with the mouth one confesses and is saved" (v. 10). There must be something that corresponds to what is going on in our heart in our confession, such that our confession shows who we truly are.

3. **A.**

   While the great day of the Lord is in view in the context of Joel, whom Paul is quoting, Dr. Godfrey did not apply this great promise from Joel in such a manner. He did, however, help us to see how this promise can encourage us in our evangelism, how it can free us from fretting over doctrinal questions in Romans 9–11 by keeping Paul's main point in view, and how the use of this verse in the New Testament can provide a strong proof for Christ's deity.

4. **A.**

   The English Standard Version translates Romans 10:14 as "And how are they to believe in him of whom they have never heard?" Another way of translating this verse would be to render the phrase "of whom" as "whom," such that people do not merely hear about *Christ but hear Christ Himself in the ministry of the Word preached.*

5. **B.**
Paul was incredibly burdened for his fellow Israelites, but he also saw that Scripture was being fulfilled in the hardening that had come upon Israel. But God was not done with Israel. In fact, He was saving Israelites, and Paul was living proof of this. Though Paul does bring up the future in Romans 11, Dr. Godfrey noted that he stresses that God is right now at work saving Jews.

6. **D.**
Paul uses each of these men to teach something in Romans. He takes lessons from the lives of Abraham and David in Romans 4 and connects Adam to the work of Christ in Romans 5. In relation to the question of God's working in Israel, Paul mentions Elijah and God's promise to Elijah that He was maintaining a remnant among Israel.

18

The Unfailing Word to Israel

INTRODUCTION

God's Word had not failed and is not failing to old covenant Israel. Even right now in history, He is gathering His elect. This idea forms the core of Paul's teaching about God's work of redemption in history for both the Jews and the gentiles. In this lesson, Dr. Godfrey sorts through the difficult matters of interpretation in Romans 11 and shows us how God's Word is never failing. This truth should lead us, as it did Paul, to worship.

LEARNING GOALS

When you have finished this lesson, you should be able to:

- Explain Paul's manner of defending the criticism that he did not appreciate Israel's place in redemptive history and did not understand the Old Testament
- Identify and navigate the great interpretive question of Romans 11 concerning Israel

KEY IDEAS

- God was and is accomplishing what He originally planned to do with His old covenant people Israel in saving the elect from among them.
- Paul's primary focus in Romans 11 is on what God is doing in history *now*.
- Israel's history is the church's history, and God is saving all people through faith in Jesus Christ such that everyone who calls on Him, and only those who call on Him, will be saved.

REFLECTION & DISCUSSION QUESTIONS

Before the Video

What Do You Think?

Take a moment to answer the following questions. They will prepare you for the lecture.

- Read Romans 11:25–27. Does it sound like Paul is talking about the future? Why or why not?

- Why is the question of God's dealings with Israel so important?

Scripture Reading

But Saul, still breathing threats and murder against the disciples of the Lord, went to the high priest and asked him for letters to the synagogues at Damascus, so that if he found any belonging to the Way, men or women, he might bring them bound to Jerusalem. Now as he went on his way, he approached Damascus, and suddenly a light from heaven shone around him. And falling to the ground, he heard a voice saying to him, "Saul, Saul, why are you persecuting me?" And he said, "Who are you, Lord?" And he said, "I am Jesus, whom you are persecuting."

—Acts 9:1–5

- What is surprising about Paul's conversion? What does Paul's conversion indicate about God's will for Israel?

During the Video

Answer the following questions while you watch the video. They will guide you through the lecture.

Crucial Faith *0:00–9:53*

- What is the major interpretive question of Romans 11?

- How is God working in relation to people in history? What does this mean for gentiles? What does it mean for Jews?

God's Future Work? *9:53–25:08*

- How does Paul use the word "mystery" in his other letters and in Romans 11?

- What is Paul's basic teaching about the salvation of "all Israel" in history?

- What is the primary challenge to the interpretation that all ethnic Israel will be saved?

After the Video

Answer the following questions after you have finished the lecture. They will help you identify and summarize the major points.

- What two warnings does Paul give to the gentiles in relation to their being grafted in to the olive tree of Israel by faith?

  If you are in a group, have the members read Romans 11:17–24. Ask: What lessons can we learn from this comparison of Israel to an olive tree when we consider that the church is one organic unity? How should this work out practically in our relationships with one another?

- What danger might accompany the belief that all ethnic Israelites will be saved? How might this danger also emerge, if we are not careful, in relation to Reformed thought about salvation?

  If you are in a group, have the members review Romans 10:8–13, considering the necessity of faith for salvation. Ask: Does this passage impress upon us the responsibility of evangelism or alleviate it in light of the larger context of God's purpose of election for Israel and the nations?

- Where do Paul's emotions especially emerge in Romans 9–11? How do they progress or change?

  If you are in a group, have the members discuss how the progression of Paul's emotional expressions in Romans 9–11 can teach us how to feel toward and think about God when we encounter difficult providences or question what God is doing in our lives or the lives of others.

PRAYER

Commit what you have learned from God's Word in this lesson to prayer.

- Praise God for His just and merciful nature, extending mercy to all people.
- Confess ways that you have been sinfully prideful about being a Christian, not recognizing that even your faith was God's gift.
- Thank God for your salvation and the assurance that He is still working in the world to save all those who call on Him.
- Ask God to give you a zeal for evangelism for the lost, knowing that faith comes through hearing.

REVIEW QUIZ

Use these multiple-choice questions to measure what you learned from this lesson.

1. Who is the primary example that Paul uses to demonstrate that God was saving Israel?
   a. Abraham
   b. David
   c. Paul
   d. Peter

2. Romans 9–11 does not provide us with comfort in our wrestling with the doctrine of election or our own spiritual condition.
   a. True
   b. False

3. What was called the *dynamic of history*?
   a. Election
   b. Faith
   c. Hope
   d. Providence

4. What word makes some people think that Paul is referring to the future salvation of Israel in Romans 11?
   a. Mystery
   b. Now
   c. Until
   d. Both a and c

5. What word can be scrutinized because of textual variation among ancient manuscripts?
   a. Mystery
   b. Now
   c. Until
   d. Both b and c

6. What other letter from Paul especially illuminates what he means by the word "mystery"?
   a. 1 Corinthians
   b. Galatians
   c. Ephesians
   d. Philippians

Answer Key—The Unfailing Word to Israel

REFLECTION & DISCUSSION QUESTIONS

Before the Video

What Do You Think?

These are personal questions. The answers should be based on your own knowledge and experience.

Scripture Reading

- What is surprising about Paul's conversion? What does Paul's conversion indicate about God's will for Israel?

  The nature of Paul's encounter with the risen Lord in blinding light is itself surprising, but it is also surprising that Paul was on his way to further persecute Christians when he was converted—a true wonder of God's mercy (see 1 Tim. 1:13). Paul was himself a Jew, so he is an example of God's continued saving work among His people.

During the Video

Crucial Faith

- What is the major interpretive question of Romans 11?

  When people think of Romans 11, they typically think of Israel and what's in store for Israel in the future. But whether Paul is speaking about the future is the major interpretive question of the text: Is Paul talking about what God will do with the Jews in the future, or is Paul talking about what God is doing with the Jews in the present?

- How is God working in relation to people in history? What does this mean for gentiles? What does it mean for Jews?

  Faith is the instrument through which we lay hold of salvation. Faith is the dynamic of history. Our relationship with God is set in terms of our faith or lack thereof. Yet faith itself is a gift from God. It is not something that we can boast in. This was a great lesson for the gentiles in Paul's day. They could not boast over unbelieving Israel on account of their faith. Just as the gentiles were given the gift of faith, God could just as easily bestow this gift upon individual Jews. Because God works in relation to faith, Paul calls the Israelites once again to faith.

God's Future Work?

- How does Paul use the word "mystery" in his other letters and in Romans 11?

Paul does not use the word "mystery" to refer to some uncertain future time in Scripture. The word "mystery" is used in reference to what was already unfolding and being revealed in his present day as the gospel went out to the gentiles. As Paul teaches in his letter to the Ephesians, the gentiles are now included in the commonwealth of Israel (see 2:11–3:6).

- What is Paul's basic teaching about the salvation of "all Israel" in history?

  Paul does not envision a salvation that is set apart for some future time for Israel. He teaches that all Israel, by which he means true Israel (see Rom. 9:6), will be saved through the whole history of the church in the preaching of the gospel. It is through this preaching that elect Jews come to faith.

- What is the primary challenge to the interpretation that all ethnic Israel will be saved?

  The Bible does not teach that all ethnic Jews will be saved, though Paul uses the phrase "all Israel will be saved" in Romans 11:26. If all ethnic Jews were in focus here, then the Bible would contradict itself. We must remember that the focus of Romans 9–11 is the statement that "everyone who calls on the name of the Lord will be saved" (10:13). No one is saved apart from faith in Jesus Christ.

After the Video

- What two warnings does Paul give to the gentiles in relation to their being grafted in to the olive tree of Israel by faith?

  Paul warned the gentiles of being prideful over being ingrafted to the olive tree of Israel. The gentiles were to understand that faith itself was a gift and that they were unnatural branches that were grafted in to this tree. The natural branches of Israel could easily be grafted back in to the tree. Contrary to a spirit of pride, Paul calls his gentile readers to fear, warning them that God could just as easily break off unnatural branches from the tree if they proved to be without faith: "Note then the kindness and the severity of God: severity toward those who have fallen, but God's kindness to you, provided you continue in his kindness. Otherwise you too will be cut off" (Rom. 11:22).

- What danger might accompany the belief that all ethnic Israelites will be saved? How might this danger also emerge, if we are not careful, in relation to Reformed thought about salvation?

  If someone believed that God would ultimately save all ethnic Israelites or even a majority of them at some future date, he or she must acknowledge a danger: if we put too much emphasis on what God may do for Israel in the future, then we might lose passion to preach the gospel to Jews today. Scripture tells us that today is "the day of salvation" (2 Cor. 6:2). Likewise, Scripture also teaches God's sovereignty in salvation, that He elects and grants faith to all who will be saved, yet we must not fail to share the gospel, believing by mistake that we have no role in God's gathering of His elect.

- Where do Paul's emotions especially emerge in Romans 9–11? How do they progress or change?

  In the beginning of this section in Romans, Paul is in distress over Israel, even wishing himself cut off for their sake. By the end of this section, Paul finds himself praising God, moving from distress to doxology. Paul begins by wishing that history had been different, but by the end of Romans 11, he is content to let God act according to His own wisdom and purpose, confident in God's mercy and recognizing that all things are working for His glory. He ends by sharing the joy that he had realized in wrestling through the same questions he was addressing for the Romans.

REVIEW QUIZ

1. **C.**
   Paul points to himself as evidence that God was at work among the Israelites. Though a partial hardening had come upon Israel, God was still saving His elect, and Paul was living proof: "I ask, then, has God rejected his people? By no means! For I myself am an Israelite, a descendant of Abraham, a member of the tribe of Benjamin" (Rom. 11:1).

2. **B.**
   We must remember the chiastic structure of Romans 9–11 and what is at the center: "Everyone who calls on the name of the Lord will be saved" (10:13). No matter our wrestling over the doctrine of election or our doubts about whether we or someone else we know and love are elect, we can rest on the truth that God saves everyone who calls on Him.

3. **B.**
   Dr. Godfrey called faith the dynamic of history *because faith is central in determining whether a person is grafted in to God's saving purpose and covenant community or cut off from that community.*

4. **D.**
   The word "until" in Romans 11:25 has strong temporal connotations in English that cause many to think that Paul must be referring to the future in this verse, but there are other ways of translating this Greek preposition. The word "mystery" also makes people think that Paul is referring to the future as if he were about to uncover for us what would take place, but Paul often uses this word elsewhere to refer to the ingrafting of the gentiles that was already taking place in his day.

5. **C.**
   "A partial hardening has come upon Israel, until the fullness of the Gentiles has come in. And in this way all Israel will be saved" (Rom. 11:25–26). The word "until"

makes us think temporally of Israel's future salvation, but this can also be translated "in order that." The occurrence of the word "now" can be used to support the idea that Israel is now being saved and that God's Word has not failed them (v. 31).

6. **C.**
   Ephesians was referenced to explain what Paul ordinarily means when he uses the word "mystery," since this letter has a special focus on the church, united—Jew and gentile—in Christ. Christ has brought down the wall between Jew and gentile (see 2:11–22), and Paul was an Apostle of this mystery that was revealed (see 3:1–6).

19

Living Sacrifices

INTRODUCTION

Knowing who we are in Christ helps us know how to love others. United to Christ, we have died to sin and are raised with Him in newness of life. Instead of letting sin reign in our mortal bodies, we present them as living sacrifices to God, and this directly connects to how we relate to others. In this lesson, Dr. Godfrey begins the last major section of Paul's letter and introduces his call for us as the church to love and serve one another in a way that is unlike the world.

LEARNING GOALS

When you have finished this lesson, you should be able to:

- Explain how Romans 12–15 is organized and connected to other sections in Paul's letter
- Understand how language about the old covenant sacrificial system can be applied to the Christian life
- Recognize the motives that Paul provides for humility toward one another

KEY IDEAS

- Features within Romans 11–15 give us clues that it can be read as a chiasm, which indicates its rich organization, and it connects thematically to other parts of Paul's letter.
- The call not to be conformed to the world is a call to be conformed to the Son.
- The whole of the Christian life can be described as a priestly service to God.
- As Christians, each a part of the one body of Christ, we need one another.

REFLECTION & DISCUSSION QUESTIONS

Before the Video

What Do You Think?

Take a moment to answer the following questions. They will prepare you for the lecture.

- What is difficult about loving others and living a life of service?

- In what ways are you in conformity to the world? What can you do to renew your mind?

Scripture Reading

So if there is any encouragement in Christ, any comfort from love, any participation in the Spirit, any affection and sympathy, complete my joy by being of the same mind, having the same love, being in full accord and of one mind. Do nothing from selfish ambition or conceit, but in humility count others more significant than yourselves. Let each of you look not only to his own interests, but also to the interests of others.

—Philippians 2:1–4

- How does Paul motivate the Philippians to love and unity in this passage?

During the Video

Answer the following questions while you watch the video. They will guide you through the lecture.

The Structure of Romans 12–15 *0:00–4:46*

- What makes commentators frustrated about Romans 12–15? What does Dr. Godfrey believe about the structure of Paul's thought in this section?

- What is the primary thing that Paul is calling us to in Romans 12–15?

Presenting Our Bodies *4:46–18:16*

- What is significant about Paul's use of the word "bodies" in Romans 12:1?

- How are we to present our bodies as living sacrifices?

Our Great Motive *18:16–24:57*

- What is the great motive in our relations with other Christians?

- What is an important implication of this great motive?

After the Video

Answer the following questions after you have finished the lecture. They will help you identify and summarize the major points.

- What reason does Paul appeal to for our living a renewed life? What great problem does Paul identify in Romans 12 in how we relate to other Christians? Is this something that you struggle with? If so, how so?

  If you are in a group, have the members read Philippians 2:1–11. Ask: What does Christ's example call us to? Why is it so radical, and how should this affect our striving to follow Christ's example?
- What do the old covenant temple sacrifices point to? What do these mean for us?

  If you are in a group, have the members discuss the idea that worship is something that we do in all of life. Ask: How does this make you think of Lord's Day worship? As something less or more significant? Why?
- In addition to driving us to humility, how should Paul's analogy of the church as a body shape how we relate to and think about other Christians?

  If you are in a group, have the members consider their unique giftings as well as the giftings of others, and have them share what they've identified.

PRAYER

Commit what you have learned from God's Word in this lesson to prayer.

- Praise God for His creativity in uniquely gifting each of His image bearers.
- Confess ways that you have thought more highly of yourself than of others.
- Thank God for raising up faithful people in the church not only to lead but to serve.

- Ask God to help you reflect on His many mercies to you in Christ so that the Spirit might work in your living a life of renewal that is marked by humility, service, and love.

REVIEW QUIZ

Use these multiple-choice questions to measure what you learned from this lesson.

1. What repeated idea clued Dr. Godfrey in to the notion that Romans 12–15 is a chiasm?
   a. Humility
   b. Judgment
   c. Love
   d. Mercy
2. What is Paul's central call in Romans 12–15?
   a. Have humility like Christ.
   b. Exercise judgment with mercy.
   c. Love the brethren and serve one another.
   d. Be content and faithful in where the Lord has you.
3. The body is the seat of sin.
   a. True
   b. False
4. What does the Greek term commonly used for "worship" mean in Romans 12:1?
   a. Kneeling down
   b. Prostrating oneself
   c. Praise
   d. Service
5. The idea that worship is in all of life often makes people think that Lord's Day worship isn't required, but there isn't a tension between these two things.
   a. True
   b. False
6. What adjective is connected with love in Romans 12?
   a. Cheerful
   b. Genuine
   c. Generous
   d. Zealous

Answer Key—Living Sacrifices

REFLECTION & DISCUSSION QUESTIONS

Before the Video

What Do You Think?

These are personal questions. The answers should be based on your own knowledge and experience.

Scripture Reading

- How does Paul motivate the Philippians to love and unity in this passage?

  In this passage, Paul appeals to the Philippian believers' experience of the blessings of Paul's ministry to them or to the blessings that they have already experienced generally as Christians: "encouragement in Christ, . . . comfort from love, . . . participation in the Spirit." Because of these realities, they are to love one another in humility. Paul even appeals to them that this would complete his joy, and he provides in the following verses our greatest example of humility: Jesus Christ (see Phil. 2:5–11).

During the Video

The Structure of Romans 12–15

- What makes commentators frustrated about Romans 12–15? What does Dr. Godfrey believe about the structure of Paul's thought in this section?

  Commentators often observe that Paul's thought does not seem to be organized in any particular way, and because good commentators hope to provide insight into a biblical text, this can be frustrating. Dr. Godfrey, however, believes that Paul's thought is organized and has carefully arranged Romans 12–15 into a chiasm.

- What is the primary thing that Paul is calling us to in Romans 12–15?

  The message of Romans 12–15 can be summarized in a succinct way: "Think about who you are. In light of who you are, love the brethren and serve one another." Because this simple message is difficult to live out, Paul develops this idea at length in Romans 12–15.

Presenting Our Bodies

- What is significant about Paul's use of the word "bodies" in Romans 12:1?

  Paul calls us to present our "bodies" as living sacrifices in Romans 12:1. This use of the word "bodies" ought to bring back to our minds all that Paul has said about the body in Romans 6–8 and especially the theme that Paul introduced in Romans 6: "Let not sin therefore reign in your mortal body" (v. 12).

- How are we to present our bodies as living sacrifices?

  Immediately after Paul calls us to present our bodies as living sacrifices, he calls us to not be conformed to the world. This entails the renewing of our minds that comes through discerning God's will in our lives through His Word, which reveals what is good, acceptable, and perfect to Him. The idea is that if we think the right way, then we will live the right way.

Our Great Motive

- What is the great motive in our relations with other Christians?

  Our great motive for how we ought to relate to other Christians is love. Paul commands, "Let love be genuine" (Rom. 12:9). Love is what binds us together as Christians. It is what we ought to strive for and what is a help to us in every one of our interactions. We cannot fulfill all that God calls us to do together as a church without love for one another.

- What is an important implication of this great motive?

  The call to love one another has a great implication. It communicates the idea that we need one another and, further, that we will be gathering with one another. The call to love one another cannot be fulfilled if we aren't making the church our community. We cannot love *one another if we do not* know *one another.*

After the Video

- What reason does Paul appeal to for our living a renewed life? What great problem does Paul identify in Romans 12 in how we relate to other Christians in Romans 12? Is this something that you struggle with? If so, how so?

  Paul calls us to a life of renewal by appealing to the mercies of God. The mercies of God can be understood as all that has come before Romans 12—God's mercy to sinners, His mercy in Christ, His mercy in sanctification, and His mercy in election. Understanding God's mercies to us can help us overcome the great problem and besetting sin of thinking more highly of ourselves than we ought. An antidote to this is renewing our minds by dwelling on the mercies of God. We can't think too highly of ourselves if we understand our need for mercy, the greatness of God's mercy, and the cost of God's mercy—Jesus Christ.

- What do the old covenant temple sacrifices point to? What do these mean for us?

  Ultimately, the old covenant temple sacrifices and the entire sacrificial system pointed forward to the one perfect (without spot or blemish) sacrifice of Jesus Christ. But for us, the holy offerings that were required also provide a picture of what holiness looks like for the people of God after Christ's ultimate sacrifice. In this sense, we are living sacrifices, giving our whole lives to spiritual service to the Lord. The word "worship" that Paul uses in Romans 12:1 is the same word used for the religious service in the temple. We partake in this in our striving after holiness, putting to death the old man and bringing to life the new man in Jesus Christ, especially in our love and service of our brothers and sisters in Christ.

- In addition to driving us to humility, how should Paul's analogy of the church as a body shape how we relate to and think about other Christians?

  Paul calls us to humility and sober judgment in how we esteem ourselves in relation to others by helping us to see that we are one body in Jesus Christ. Paul makes an analogy between the church and a body: just as one body has many parts, so, too, the church is filled with many people with many gifts, each serving a different function but for the sake of the whole. This reality should not lead us to envy others or to think more highly of ourselves because of our respective giftings. But just as the body needs its many parts, we need one another as the church. Just as the body as a whole would suffer if its parts were neglected, so, too, the church would suffer if people were not valued or were marginalized.

REVIEW QUIZ

1. **B.**
   Chiasm is a literary structure that frames a main idea. Often, when two ideas are repeated in a section of Scripture, there may be a chiastic structure. Sometimes, identifying this repeated idea provides enough of a lead for one to see how other ideas are repeated as well. For example, Dr. Godfrey first noticed that Paul talks about judgment in Romans 12:19 and in 14:12, cluing him in to the possibility of a chiasm.

2. **C.**
   The message of Romans 12–15 is in one sense simple but in another sense difficult. Paul's call to us is to think about who we are and out of that to love and serve our brothers and sisters in Christ. It's a simple message, but it is hard to live out, which is why Paul spends chapters developing it.

3. **B.**
   Though Paul calls us to present our bodies as living sacrifices, the body isn't to be thought of as a seat of sin. The body is, however, a constant reminder of sin. Dr. Godfrey called it the "sign" of sin.

4. **D.**
   Two main words are used for the concept of worship in the Bible. One communicates something about the general posture of worship in kneeling down or prostrating oneself. The other is often translated "service" and refers to the service that was offered in the temple, which is what is in view in Romans 12:1.

5. **A.**

It is not uncommon for people to think that the type of sacrificial life that Christians are to lead and what Paul calls "worship" means that gathering to worship with other Christians isn't required or isn't a main priority. These two things are not in tension with each other. Paul is calling us not to be conformed to the world, and it does not make sense that such a thing would include not gathering with God's people to worship.

6. **B.**

In Romans 12:9, Paul says, "Let love be genuine." Each of the other concepts appears in Romans 12, but they relate to the manner in which we ought to use our gifts in the church. For instance, we are to do acts of mercy with cheerfulness, to lead with zeal, and to contribute generously.

20

The Life of Love

INTRODUCTION

Romans provides us with instruction for living lives of love both inside and outside the Christian community. While the reason for Paul's transition from talking about how Christians are to love one another to how they are to relate to civil authority may not seem apparent, they are both connected to Christians' posture toward God as the ultimate authority. In this lesson, Dr. Godfrey traces Paul's thought in Romans 12–13 and draws practical implications for our lives in the present moment before the return of Christ.

LEARNING GOALS

When you have finished this lesson, you should be able to:

- Summarize Paul's teaching on what love looks like among Christians
- Explain how Paul's teaching about how Christians are to relate to one another connects to how we are to relate to civil authorities
- Identify the central part of Paul's practical instruction in Romans 12–15

KEY IDEAS

- Love expressed through patience sometimes means enduring injustice.
- God has established civil government as an institution to keep order in the world.
- A faithful servant-leader submits to authority and accepts the work required of him or her.
- We are called to not take vengeance in our own hands and to submit to the authorities that God has ordained as we wait for Christ to make all things new.

REFLECTION & DISCUSSION QUESTIONS

Before the Video

What Do You Think?

Take a moment to answer the following questions. They will prepare you for the lecture.

- What is most needed if we are to rightly love God and our neighbors?
- Is the call to honor civil authorities difficult for you to accept? Why or why not?

Scripture Reading

If then you have been raised with Christ, seek the things that are above, where Christ is, seated at the right hand of God. Set your minds on things that are above, not on things that are on earth. For you have died, and your life is hidden with Christ in God. When Christ who is your life appears, then you also will appear with him in glory. Put to death therefore what is earthly in you: sexual immorality, impurity, passion, evil desire, and covetousness, which is idolatry. On account of these the wrath of God is coming.

—Colossians 3:1–6

- What is a unifying motivation for setting our minds on the things above and putting to death what is earthly in us?

During the Video

Answer the following questions while you watch the video. They will guide you through the lecture.

Loving Fellow Christians *0:00–8:45*

- What two things does Dr. Godfrey identify as "difficult"?
- Why does Paul call us not to seek our own vengeance? What is the failure of liberal Christianity related to justice and judgment?

Honoring Civil Authorities *8:45–17:39*

- How does Paul describe the civil authority and civil governors in Romans 13?

- What does Dr. Godfrey identify as a problem in our day? Describe this problem.

At the Center *17:39–24:32*

- What is at the center of the letter structure of Romans 12–15?

- How do Colossians 3 and the Heidelberg Catechism speak about how we are to live?

After the Video

Answer the following questions after you have finished the lecture. They will help you identify and summarize the major points.

- What is a temptation when we encounter lists of commands in the Bible? How ought we to read them?

  If you are in a group, have the members read Romans 12:9–15. Ask: What would be required to read this passage with reasonable care? Do these verses help you identify areas in your life where repentance is needed?

- How do Paul's commands about our not seeking vengeance as Christians relate to his commands about honoring civil authorities?

  If you are in a group, have the members discuss some of the issues in recent years that have caused difficulties related to the issue of civil authority. Ask: How does Dr. Godfrey's explanation of Romans 13 help you understand this issue better?

- How does Paul summarize the law in Romans 13? How does this echo Christ's teaching when He was confronted by the Pharisees?

  If you are in a group, have the members read Galatians 5:13–25. Ask: What connections can you make to Paul's teaching in this passage to Dr. Godfrey's explanation of Romans 12:14–13:14?

PRAYER

Commit what you have learned from God's Word in this lesson to prayer.

- Praise God as the Almighty who has all power and authority.

- Confess times when you have disparaged or disregarded civil authorities as instituted by God.
- Thank God for the order and stability that is provided by just civil governments.
- Ask God to enable you by the Holy Spirit to walk in the light as one who has "put on the Lord Jesus Christ" (Rom. 13:14).

REVIEW QUIZ

Use these multiple-choice questions to measure what you learned from this lesson.

1. Paul's comments on being subject to governing authorities must be understood as referring to Christian governments.
   a. True
   b. False

2. Which theologian said that the worst thing that can happen for human society is the collapse of all government?
   a. Charles Spurgeon
   b. Thomas Müntzer
   c. Martin Luther
   d. John Calvin

3. What word is used to describe a ruler as God's "servant"?
   a. Slave
   b. Elder
   c. Deacon
   d. Caesar

4. In addition to "for the sake of conscience," what is the other reason given for our subjection to governing authorities in Romans 13:5?
   a. The approval of the ruler
   b. The peace of the church
   c. The witness of the gospel
   d. The wrath of God

5. Subjecting to governing authorities does not mean that we can't pursue better legislation as citizens.
   a. True
   b. False

6. What theological topic was related to not seeking vengeance and honoring governing authorities?
   a. Anthropology
   b. Christology
   c. Doxology
   d. Eschatology

Answer Key—The Life of Love

REFLECTION & DISCUSSION QUESTIONS

Before the Video

What Do You Think?

These are personal questions. The answers should be based on your own knowledge and experience.

Scripture Reading

- What is a unifying motivation for setting our minds on the things above and putting to death what is earthly in us?

  In both these admonitions, the return of Christ and the coming judgment of God are provided as appeals to think on that which is above and to put to death that which is earthly. Even greater than these is the reality that we are already dead to sin such that our lives are hidden in Christ. We still put sin to death, however, knowing that we will one day be like Him and without sin, which God will judge, when He returns.

During the Video

Loving Fellow Christians

- What two things does Dr. Godfrey identify as "difficult"?

  In Romans 12, Paul is calling us to live in community as Christians harmoniously, humbly, and peaceably. The summary statement of this section deals with our living peaceably with all. *But this is a difficult task, and we need God's gracious renewal to do it. Paul calls us to another difficult task: to never avenge ourselves. When we have been truly sinned against, used, or unjustly persecuted, it is hard not to strike out in retaliation.*

- Why does Paul call us not to seek our own vengeance? What is the failure of liberal Christianity related to justice and judgment?

  Paul calls us not to seek our own vengeance fundamentally because vengeance is the Lord's. Perfect justice and judgment belong to God. Instead, we are to love our enemies. Liberal Christianity extends this principle too far in denying that judgment is a reality, in not calling sin "sin," or in thinking that love will ultimately mean that judgment will not occur and that God will set aside His justice.

Honoring Civil Authorities

- How does Paul describe the civil authority and civil governors in Romans 13?

Paul describes civil authority as something appointed and instituted by God. For that reason, we must be subject to governing authorities. Rulers are even described as God's servants. The word used in Romans 13:4 for "servant" is the same word that designates the church office of a deacon.

- What does Dr. Godfrey identify as a problem in our day? Describe this problem.

  The problem that was identified is a spirit of lawlessness that is on display in our day. This is manifested in an attitude to government wherein people feel obligated to obey only the laws that are agreeable to them. It is an abuse of freedom to attack and not honor civil government, but we can strive to change laws and make them more just.

At the Center

- What is at the center of the letter structure of Romans 12–15?

  At the center of Romans 12–15 is Paul's call to us to know the time so that we remain awake and watchful. It can be said that the world lives asleep, not acknowledging that we are in the last days. Paul says that the night is gone and that the day is at hand, the day of the Lord's appearing. As Christians, we must not fall back into the ways of the world but keep striving for holiness in anticipation of that day.

- How do Colossians 3 and the Heidelberg Catechism speak about how we are to live?

  Echoing Paul's command in Romans 13:14 to "put on the Lord Jesus Christ," the Heidelberg Catechism talks about sanctification in terms of putting off and putting on—putting off the old man and putting on the new man. Likewise, Paul makes the same point in Colossians to "put off the old self" and to "put on the new self" (3:9–10).

After the Video

- What is a temptation when we encounter lists of commands in the Bible? How ought we to read them?

  Lists in the Bible can make us speed through them in our reading. This is perhaps a greater temptation in a list of names, but it also happens with lists of exhortations, sins, or giftings that God gives to Christians. We might think that these things are so clear that they don't need to be explained and that we don't need to slow down for them. But even if a call to love our neighbors, for example, sounds simple, actually loving our neighbors isn't. Some of the most difficult things to do are not hard to understand, but we ought to slow down and take time to assess our lives as to how we are living up to what Scripture is calling us to. These lists are opportunities to ask: "Where am I in my life? Where is the Lord calling me? What gifts has the Lord given me?"

- How do Paul's commands about our not seeking vengeance as Christians relate to his commands about honoring civil authorities?

  Both God and civil authorities exercise judgment and preserve justice. We do not seek vengeance because vengeance is the Lord's, and He has instituted civil government to maintain judgment and justice in this world. One of the reasons that we are called not to take justice away from God or the civil government is that we might find, through such action, that we are the ones who are judged. Honoring civil authorities assures us that we do not become condemned in wrongdoing, and because civil authorities are described as servants of God, honoring them is a way of honoring God and His claim on justice.

- How does Paul summarize the law in Romans 13? How does this echo Christ's teaching when He was confronted by the Pharisees?

  Paul summarizes the law in Romans 13 in one word: "love." Paul says, "The one who loves another has fulfilled the law" (v. 8.) When Jesus was confronted by the Pharisees in Matthew 22, they asked Him about the greatest commandment, and He summarized it as the love of God—and He added something to this answer that the Pharisees might not have expected to be confronted with: the love of neighbor. The Pharisees claimed to love and honor God, but as they so often displayed, they hate their neighbors. But love comprises the entirety of the law.

REVIEW QUIZ

1. **B.**
   Paul was writing to Christians in Rome, at the heart of an empire that was not Christian and that had crucified the Lord. He called them to honor the emperor. To hear the call to us from Romans 13, we must understand that we, too, must honor civil authorities in our own contexts, adhering to laws and paying taxes that are owed.

2. **C.**
   Paul tells us that civil authorities have been instituted by God and that they are even His servants in judgment and justice. If we did not have these authorities, there would be chaos. Luther understood this, and that is why he said that the collapse of all government and chaos would be the worst thing for a society.

3. **C.**
   Two words are used to describe civil authorities that may be surprising to us. The word "ministers" is used, a word that brings to mind temple service. The word "servant" is also used, diakonon, *and this word is translated elsewhere in Scripture as "deacon."*

4. **D.**
   The way that Christians respond to the authorities that God has instituted can contribute to the witness of the gospel, the peace of the church, or even favor. The other

reason that Paul gives, however, for honoring civil authorities is the wrath of God because violating the law comes with judgment.

5. **A.**
   Whenever possible, Christians are permitted to seek after just legislation. Subjection to governing authorities is a call not to passivity but to law-abiding citizenship under the authorities that God has put in place.

6. **D.**
   Though imperfectly, justice is rendered now through civil government, but one day, God will bring perfect justice into the world. Not seeking retaliation and honoring civil authority is a matter of eschatology. We await the return of Jesus Christ but also subject ourselves to the order that God has established now.

21

The Lordship of Christ

INTRODUCTION

As Christians, we are called to "put on" the Lord Jesus Christ. One of the ways that this can manifest itself is our charity toward other believers. Romans 14 is famous for its discussion of the weaker and the stronger brother on issues of Christian conscience. In this lesson, Dr. Godfrey explains what type of issues Paul is identifying as matters of Christian conscience and why we ought not to judge fellow believers on these matters: Jesus is Lord, and every one of us must give an account to Him.

LEARNING GOALS

When you have finished this lesson, you should be able to:

- Understand the seriousness of division in the church
- Describe what matters are and are not in view in Paul's teaching about the stronger and weaker brothers
- Explain how we ought to respond to differences with other believers

KEY IDEAS

- The life of love diverts its attention away from the flesh and to Christ as Lord.
- Paul addresses differences of opinion about promoting piety in Romans 14.
- In our disagreements with one another, we are called to love and honor one another, maintaining the peace that God has created among us.

REFLECTION & DISCUSSION QUESTIONS

Before the Video

What Do You Think?

Take a moment to answer the following questions. They will prepare you for the lecture.

- Why is division in the church a serious matter?

- When is it appropriate to disagree and take a hard stance over matters of the faith?

Scripture Reading

I do not ask for these only, but also for those who will believe in me through their word, that they may all be one, just as you, Father, are in me, and I in you, that they also may be in us, so that the world may believe that you have sent me. The glory that you have given me I have given to them, that they may be one even as we are one, I in them and you in me, that they may become perfectly one, so that the world may know that you sent me and loved them even as you loved me.

—John 17:20–23

- What is at stake if there are divisions in the church?

During the Video

Answer the following questions while you watch the video. They will guide you through the lecture.

No Provision for the Flesh *0:00–5:44*

- How does Paul show us the seriousness of division in the church?

- How does Paul stress the lordship of Christ over our lives in Romans 13?

The Weaker and Stronger *5:44–19:52*

- What is a danger of taking Paul's statements about the weak and the strong out of context?

- What is the general difference of opinion among the weak and the strong?

The Call to Mutual Upbuilding *19:52–25:07*

- How do we avoid judgment and offense in matters of indifference?

- Whom does Paul side with, the weaker or the stronger? How does the stronger express love toward the weaker?

After the Video

Answer the following questions after you have finished the lecture. They will help you identify and summarize the major points.

- Paul is not addressing matters relating to which two areas when settling the dispute between the weaker and the stronger in Rome?

  If you are in a group, have the members think of how they would handle sin and error in the lives of other Christians. Ask: When should the principles from Romans 14 be applied?

- What specific practices in Rome is Paul addressing? What is he not dealing with?

  If you are in a group, have the members scan Romans 14 and draw out the statements that emphasize God's supremacy and Christ's lordship over believers.

- What are some of the examples of matters of indifference that were provided by Dr. Godfrey? What other examples can you think of? How are we to handle matters of indifference?

  If you are in a group, have the members discuss any personal experience in dealing with disputes among Christians. Ask: What was successful in achieving peace? What was unsuccessful?

PRAYER

Commit what you have learned from God's Word in this lesson to prayer.

- Praise God as the One to whom all must give an account on the day of Christ.
- Confess ways that you have judged other Christians concerning matters of indifference.
- Thank God for the freedom of conscience that we have in serving the Lord Jesus Christ.
- Ask God to work by the Spirit to maintain and help you work toward maintaining the bonds of peace in your local church.

REVIEW QUIZ

Use these multiple-choice questions to measure what you learned from this lesson.

1. Who was converted after reading from Romans 13?
   a. Charles Spurgeon
   b. Martin Luther
   c. Augustine of Hippo
   d. Jonathan Edwards

2. What best summarizes the context of Paul's statements about the weak and the strong in the structure of Romans 12–15?
   a. God's moral law
   b. Jew-gentile relations
   c. Judgment
   d. Sanctification

3. Which of the following does *not* identify what's at the heart of the dispute between the weak and the strong?
   a. God's moral law
   b. Jewish dietary restrictions
   c. Justification
   d. All of the above

4. Paul's teaching about the weak and the strong implies that we ought not to ever criticize or correct another Christian.
   a. True
   b. False

5. Romans 14:5 has been used to deny the enduring nature of the Sabbath day.
   a. True
   b. False

6. Which of the following completes this verse: "The one who observes the day, observes it . . ."?
   a. ". . . as a weaker brother."
   b. ". . . as a stronger brother."
   c. ". . . in honor of the Lord."
   d. ". . . in thanks to God."

Answer Key—The Lordship of Christ

REFLECTION & DISCUSSION QUESTIONS

Before the Video

What Do You Think?

These are personal questions. The answers should be based on your own knowledge and experience.

Scripture Reading

- What is at stake if there are divisions in the church?

  John 17 captures Jesus' prayer for us, and a key feature of that prayer is His desire for our unity, a unity similar to the unity between the Father and the Son. This unity serves a purpose: that the world would believe that the Father sent the Son and that the church is uniquely loved. Division in the church works against Jesus' will for the church as Lord.

During the Video

No Provision for the Flesh

- How does Paul show us the seriousness of division in the church?

  In Romans 13:13, Paul writes, "Let us walk properly as in the daytime, not in orgies and drunkenness, not in sexual immorality and sensuality, not in quarreling and jealousy." The seriousness of division in the church is pronounced because of the other sins with which it is listed. Just as drunkenness and sexual immorality are serious sins, so are the quarreling and jealousy that bring division in the church.

- How does Paul stress the lordship of Christ over our lives in Romans 13?

  Paul stresses Christ's lordship in Romans 13 by first calling us to "cast off" the works of darkness and to "put on" the armor of light—to "put on" the Lord Jesus Christ. Jesus is to be the Lord of our life as we seek to put to death the works of the flesh. Making Him the center of our focus is essential for our making no provisions for the flesh.

The Weaker and Stronger

- What is a danger of taking Paul's statements about the weak and the strong out of context?

  If we take Paul's statements about the weak and the strong out of context, we might walk away from Romans 14 with a misconception that we ought not to ever rightly criticize or call into question anyone in the Christian community.

- What is the general difference of opinion among the weak and the strong?

  While the difference of opinion among the weak and the strong was over specific matters relating to fasting or feasting, the main point of difference was in the Roman Christians' opinions about what would most promote piety.

The Call to Mutual Upbuilding

- How do we avoid judgment and offense in matters of indifference?

  The way that we avoid judging fellow Christians in matters of indifference as well as knowing how to act around others when we are aware of points of disagreement is through love. In Romans 14:15, this is made explicit: "For if your brother is grieved by what you eat, you are no longer walking in love. By what you eat, do not destroy the one for whom Christ died."

- Whom does Paul side with, the weaker or the stronger? How does the stronger express love toward the weaker?

  Paul addresses the strong more than the weak and calls them to "bear with the failings of the weak" (Rom. 15:1). The strong bear with the weak by not pleasing themselves, by not eating or drinking if doing so would cause the weaker to stumble.

After the Video

- Paul is not addressing matters relating to which two areas when settling the dispute between the weaker and the stronger in Rome?

  The differences between the weaker and stronger in Rome are not over matters of the moral law or over justification. No one can appeal to Romans 14 and say that he or she is a "weak Christian" as an excuse for sin. This is not the issue that Paul is addressing in Rome. Likewise, these Roman Christians were not arguing that the practices in dispute call into question someone's standing with God. Paul's warning to Timothy about people who teach abstinence from food and the like for justification in 1 Timothy 4:1–3 is a strong condemnation, but Paul does not condemn the Roman Christians because he is addressing matters of indifference when it comes to one's righteous standing before God in Christ.

- What specific practices in Rome is Paul addressing? What is he not dealing with?

  Paul is likely addressing matters related to fasting on specific days in order to encourage spiritual practice and spiritual-mindedness within the church. It was believed that abstaining from meat and wine on these days or more broadly would serve this end. There was a disagreement about this among the Roman Christians, however. Paul is not addressing Jewish dietary laws because while there was a restriction against certain meats, there was not a restriction against all meats. Just as Paul is not referring to Jewish dietary laws, Paul is not referring to Jewish days or the Christian Sabbath.

- What are some of the examples of matters of indifference that were provided by Dr. Godfrey? What other examples can you think of? How are we to handle matters of indifference?

  The matters of indifference that the Romans were dealing with related to food and drink and the observance of special days to promote piety. Drinking wine in moderation was specifically named. Dr. Godfrey also made a connection to practices such as a midweek prayer meeting. Such a practice is not a bad thing and can benefit the life of the church, but it is not required. If disputes arise about matters of indifference, we must not take up the cause of our particular right or freedom in Christ but rather love and tolerate fellow Christians, respecting their differences, over such matters. In the case of the stronger, there seems to be greater obligation for maintaining unity in the church by putting aside one's freedoms in Christ (Rom. 15:1–2).

REVIEW QUIZ

1. **C.**

   Augustine of Hippo narrates his conversion in his Confessions. *At this time in his life, he was intellectually persuaded of the faith, but he was still struggling with whether he could live as a Christian. Struggling within himself, he was converted when he opened the Scriptures to Romans 13:14 and read, "Put on the Lord Jesus Christ, and make no provision for the flesh, to gratify its desires."*

2. **C.**

   All these themes have been explored within Paul's letter. In the section of Romans 12–15, which Dr. Godfrey has identified as a chiasm, Paul's remarks concerning the stronger and the weaker are in reference to judgment, that we ought not to pass judgment on one another in matters of indifference.

3. **D.**

   Paul is addressing matters of indifference to help smooth relations between the Christians in Rome. He is not referring to issues at the heart of the Christian faith, such as justification and obedience to God's law. Also, because he discusses abstention from all meats, Jewish dietary laws are not in view.

4. **B.**

   While we are always to act out of love for one another, Paul's teaching about the weak and the strong does not mean that we can ignore sin or false teaching in the church. One could reach this conclusion only by taking Paul's comments out of context.

5. **A.**

   Romans 14:5 reads: "One person esteems one day as better than another, while another esteems all days alike. Each one should be fully convinced in his own mind." This passage has been used to deny that there is a Sabbath day in the new covenant.

6. **C.**
   We can free ourselves from judging other Christians over matters of indifference when we realize that we are all aiming to serve the Lord and that each of us will be called to give an account of our actions to Him (Rom. 14:10–12).

22

The Theme of Hope

INTRODUCTION

The Apostle Paul makes us better readers of the Old Testament in his letter to the Romans. The manner in which he quotes the Old Testament teaches us what we need to look out for when reading the Old Testament. In this lesson, Dr. Godfrey explores a primary purpose of the Old Testament that Paul outlines for us in Romans: to be encouragement to us that we might endure and have hope.

LEARNING GOALS

When you have finished this lesson, you should be able to:

- Explain Paul's use of Psalm 69 in his letter to the Romans
- Know what types of questions we should be asking when studying the Old Testament
- Trace the theme of hope through Paul's letter to the Romans
- Articulate Paul's understanding of his calling as an Apostle

KEY IDEAS

- Hope is one of the great themes of the book of Romans, and Paul even presents hope as one of the great purposes of the Old Testament.
- Paul quotes Psalm 69, an imprecatory psalm that is full of lament, in Romans 15, and his use of this psalm can help us understand endurance through trial biblically.
- The last main section of Romans ends with Paul's reflecting on the purpose and fulfillment of his ministry as something anticipated in the Old Testament.

REFLECTION & DISCUSSION QUESTIONS

Before the Video

What Do You Think?

Take a moment to answer the following questions. They will prepare you for the lecture.

- In what ways does the Old Testament point forward to Christ?

- Why is endurance important in the Christian life?

Scripture Reading

Let not those who hope in you be put to shame through me, O Lord God of hosts; let not those who seek you be brought to dishonor through me, O God of Israel. For it is for your sake that I have borne reproach, that dishonor has covered my face.

—Psalm 69:6–7

- Think of these words as the words of Christ. How might these verses give you encouragement, endurance, and hope?

During the Video

Answer the following questions while you watch the video. They will guide you through the lecture.

Psalm 69 and Endurance *0:00–11:20*

- What is the "end" of the Psalter? Explain.

- What is biblical endurance?

The Theme of Hope *11:20–16:48*

- What does hope look toward, and what is it rooted in?

- How does Paul appeal to the Lord in Romans 15:5, and what does he ask for?

Christ's Ministry, Paul's Ministry *16:48–24:40*

- How does Paul describe Christ's ministry?
- How does Paul describe his own ministry?

After the Video

Answer the following questions after you have finished the lecture. They will help you identify and summarize the major points.

- How does Paul teach us to read the Old Testament? What questions might we ask when reading the Old Testament to make the most of this important purpose of the Old Testament?

  If you are in a group, have the members read Psalm 69. Ask: What is Paul trying to teach the Romans through Jesus' experience of the cross? Are there any areas in which we can apply this to our own lives?
- Where are some places that the theme of hope is found in Paul's letter to the Romans?

  If you are in a group, have the members discuss why the hope of the Christian is better than worldly hope about the future.
- How does Paul's boldly reminding the Romans at certain points resemble the task of a pastor today? What do you need to be reminded of each Lord's Day?

  If you are in a group, have the members share what reasons they might have for needing to be reminded of the truths of the gospel every Lord's Day.

PRAYER

Commit what you have learned from God's Word in this lesson to prayer.

- Praise God as the God of encouragement and endurance who sustains you in the Christian life.
- Confess any prayerless area in your life in which you might be passionlessly enduring your trials.
- Thank God for the Old Testament as a source of encouragement for your endurance and hope in the Christian life.
- Ask God to help you grow in the knowledge and certainty that He is accomplishing His purposes in the world and in your life.

REVIEW QUIZ

Use these multiple-choice questions to measure what you learned from this lesson.

1. Psalm 69 applies only to Christ in anticipation of His experience of the cross.
   a. True
   b. False

2. What is the central verse of Psalm 69?
   a. "My eyes grow dim with waiting for my God."
   b. "The reproaches of those who reproach you have fallen on me."
   c. "Hide not your face from your servant . . . ; make haste to answer me."
   d. "For God will save Zion and build up the cities of Judah."

3. What word does *not* relate to what Psalm 69 can teach us about biblically bearing trials?
   a. Passion
   b. Passive
   c. Patience
   d. Prayer

4. How is God described in Romans 15?
   a. As the God of encouragement
   b. As the God of endurance
   c. As the God of hope
   d. All of the above

5. Paul does not sternly rebuke the Romans in his letter, but he has boldly reminded them at some points throughout his letter.
   a. True
   b. False

6. What is significant about Paul's quotations from the Old Testament about Christ's ministry for the gentiles?
   a. Paul reinterprets verses to show their deeper, unforeseen meaning.
   b. Paul shows the necessity of circumcision of the heart and not the flesh.
   c. Paul uses passages from the Law, the Writings, and the Prophets.
   d. Paul demonstrates that his ministry is also a priestly service.

Answer Key—The Theme of Hope

REFLECTION & DISCUSSION QUESTIONS

Before the Video

What Do You Think?

These are personal questions. The answers should be based on your own knowledge and experience.

Scripture Reading

- Think of these words as the words of Christ. How might these verses give you encouragement, endurance, and hope?

  We may think of these words as the words of Christ because, as Scripture, they are, and they anticipate his experience of bearing reproach for God's sake and on behalf of His people. In these words, we see Christ's desire that we should experience shame or dishonor, which He delivers us from through bearing these things for us. This teaches us what it means to endure as Christians but also prompts us to rejoice in the encouragement and hope that we receive when reflecting on the finished work of Christ.

During the Video

Psalm 69 and Endurance

- What is the "end" of the Psalter? Explain.

  The end of the Psalter is always Jesus. In the case of Psalm 69, even though King David wrote these words and experienced them, what he said applies to Jesus' experience, too, and is ultimately fulfilled in Jesus.

- What is biblical endurance?

  One way to approach this question is to consider what biblical endurance is not. It is not emotionally detached stoicism; it is something filled with passion because it involves an opening up of the heart to the Lord in prayer, waiting for His timing in patience.

The Theme of Hope

- What does hope look toward, and what is it rooted in?

  Hope looks to the future. It is future-oriented, and its foundation is God, a confidence in God that He will work out what is for our good in the future. We look to God as the "God of hope" (Rom. 15:13).

- How does Paul appeal to the Lord in Romans 15:5, and what does he ask for?

  In Romans 15:5, Paul calls on God for the sake of the church in Rome, identifying Him as "the God of endurance and encouragement." Paul asks that He unite the Romans in harmony and in one voice in glorifying God. We ask for the very things that we need to persevere in the Christian life in hope from the God who controls endurance and encouragement and who is the God of endurance and encouragement.

Christ's Ministry, Paul's Ministry

- How does Paul describe Christ's ministry?

  Paul describes Christ's ministry in terms of His being a "servant" (a "deacon") to the Jews to show that God was faithful to them and the promises that He made to the patriarchs of Israel, which always had in view with Christ's fulfillment the redemption of the gentiles (Rom. 15:8).

- How does Paul describe his own ministry?

  Paul calls himself "a minister of Christ Jesus to the Gentiles," and once again in this letter, Paul connects his work to the priestly office when he says that his ministry to the gentiles is "the priestly service of the gospel of God" (Rom. 15:16).

After the Video

- How does Paul teach us to read the Old Testament? What questions might we ask when reading the Old Testament to make the most of this important purpose of the Old Testament?

  In many ways, Paul's letter to the Romans is a defense of his right understanding of the Old Testament. One striking statement in particular stands out for teaching us an important purpose of the Old Testament for us: "For whatever was written in former days was written for our instruction, that through endurance and through the encouragement of the Scriptures we might have hope" (15:4). When we read the Old Testament, we ought to look for ways that it encourages us to endurance and hope. Some questions that we ought to ask were given as examples: "How does this Old Testament passage help us endure? How does it help us face suffering? How does it encourage us?"

- Where are some places that the theme of hope is found in Paul's letter to the Romans?

  Romans 15 gives us an opportunity to reflect on the theme of hope that is pronounced in this chapter but that can also be traced throughout the whole letter. In Romans 4, Paul characterizes Abraham and his faith as one who "in hope . . . believed against hope" (v. 18). He did not distrust God but was strong in his faith toward God's promises despite the natural things that would seem to work against them. In Romans 5, hope is revealed to be a fruit of godly suffering (vv. 3–4), and in Romans 8, we also have a great reiteration of the importance of hope as it connects to faith and patient perseverance in the Christian life.

- How does Paul's boldly reminding the Romans at certain points resemble the task of a pastor today? What do you need to be reminded of each Lord's Day?

  The Romans did not truly understand the significance of Paul's calling as the Apostle to the gentiles, nor did they understand God's purpose with the gentiles. This may have affected how others interpreted Paul's teaching about the free grace of the gospel and sanctification, also important themes in his letter. Dr. Godfrey pointed out that preachers, week by week, do a work in preaching akin to Paul's writing. We, though we may learn something afresh, are not taught something brand-new every Lord's Day. Rather, we are stirred up in the gospel by way of bold reminder.

REVIEW QUIZ

1. **B.**
   Psalm 69 was written by King David and reflects his experience. Though this psalm does anticipate Christ's experience on the cross and is indeed His psalm because it contains His words as Scripture, it is also about David.

2. **C.**
   Paul's quotation of Psalm 69 in Romans 15 concerns Christ's not pleasing Himself: "The reproaches of those who reproached you fell on me" (Rom. 15:3, quoting Ps. 69:9). Dr. Godfrey in exploring the deeper meaning of this psalm highlighted its central verse, which is often the most significant portion of many psalms: "Hide not your face from your servant, for I am in distress; make haste to answer me" (v. 17).

3. **B.**
   Far from encouraging us to be stoic or passive in our suffering, the Bible provides us with pictures of faithful bearing up under trial and passionate patience in prayer. We see this model from the psalmist in Psalm 69.

4. **D.**
   In Romans 15:5, Paul appeals to God for the Christians in Rome: "May the God of endurance and encouragement grant you to live in such harmony with one another, in accord with Christ Jesus." In Romans 15:13, Paul appeals again to God as the "God of hope."

5. **A.**
   Paul said: "I myself am satisfied about you, my brothers, that you yourselves are full of goodness, filled with all knowledge and able to instruct one another. But on some points I have written to you very boldly by way of reminder" (Rom. 15:14–15). Paul wrote boldly especially about Jew-gentile relations as the Apostle to the gentiles, not to prioritize one group over another but to promote the unity of the church.

6. **C.**
In defending his understanding of the Old Testament and the anticipated salvation of the gentiles in the Old Testament that would come through Christ, Paul quotes from every part of the Hebrew Scriptures, from Deuteronomy (from the Law), from 2 Samuel (from the Writings), and from Isaiah (from the Prophets).

23

Paul's Conclusion

INTRODUCTION

Paul concludes his letter to the Romans by returning to some of the main themes of the letter and extending heartfelt greetings to the congregation. Before addressing particular individuals in the church, Paul again defends his ministry and his teachings on obedience, and he provides reasons for why he has been delayed in coming to Rome. In this lesson, Dr. Godfrey brings this teaching series to an end by looking at Paul's heart for the Christians in Rome.

LEARNING GOALS

When you have finished this lesson, you should be able to:

- Identify major themes of Paul's letter in his concluding section
- Provide details about some of the people that Paul names at the end of his letter
- Explain distinctive features and challenges related to Paul's final greetings

KEY IDEAS

- Paul never loses the thread of his thought throughout the whole letter to the Romans.
- Paul's final greetings demonstrate that women play a crucial role in the ministry of the church but do not necessarily provide evidence that women may hold the office of elder or deacon.
- Paul ends his letter to the Romans in the most appropriate way—glorifying God.

REFLECTION & DISCUSSION QUESTIONS

Before the Video

What Do You Think?

Take a moment to answer the following questions. They will prepare you for the lecture.

- What major theme of Paul's letter has been most impactful to learn about for you?

- Concluding this letter, would you consider Romans to be Paul's magnum opus, as it is often called?

Scripture Reading

Of this gospel I was made a minister according to the gift of God's grace, which was given me by the working of his power. To me, though I am the very least of all the saints, this grace was given, to preach to the Gentiles the unsearchable riches of Christ, and to bring to light for everyone what is the plan of the mystery hidden for ages in God, who created all things, so that through the church the manifold wisdom of God might now be made known to the rulers and authorities in the heavenly places. This was according to the eternal purpose that he has realized in Christ Jesus our Lord, in whom we have boldness and access with confidence through our faith in him.

—Ephesians 3:7–12

- How was the "mystery" of God revealed?

During the Video

Answer the following questions while you watch the video. They will guide you through the lecture.

Major Themes *0:00–8:22*

- How does Paul reemphasize to the Romans that he is not antinomian in his teaching?

- What reasons does Paul give for not having yet visited the church in Rome? Why is he eager to visit soon?

Phoebe and Junia *8:22–16:00*

- How does Paul describe Phoebe? Did she hold this office in the church?

- How does Paul describe Junia? Did she hold this office in the church?

Final Blessings *16:00–23:19*

- How does Paul end his final instruction to the Romans for unity in confidence and hope?

- How can "the only wise God" (Rom. 16:27) be thought of as Paul's parting encouragement to the Romans and to us?

After the Video

Answer the following questions after you have finished the lecture. They will help you identify and summarize the major points.

- How might Paul have impressed upon the Romans their need to be concerned for poor and suffering Christians? How ought we to minister to such Christians?

  If you are in a group, have the members discuss whether they have a better understanding of the unity of Paul's letter to the Romans.

- Why might Paul's personal greeting to the Romans be so extensive?

  If you are in a group, have the members read Paul's full greetings in Romans 16:1–16. Ask: What stands out to you?

- As you reflect on your experience in studying Paul's letter to the Romans in this teaching series, what concepts, verses, or passages have most significantly shaped your understanding of this letter?

  If you are in a group, have the members read Romans 1:1–6 and 16:25–27. Ask: What are the common elements in these two passages? In conclusion, have them discuss their answers to the main question above.

PRAYER

Commit what you have learned from God's Word in this lesson to prayer.

- Praise God as the only wise God.
- Confess any ways that you fail to encourage fellow Christians in their service to the Lord.
- Thank God for making you a part of His church, uniting you to Christ and to fellow workers by the Holy Spirit.
- Ask God to equip you with an encouraging word for members in your church for their service to the Lord.

REVIEW QUIZ

Use these multiple-choice questions to measure what you learned from this lesson.

1. All except for which of the following themes does Paul address at the end of his letter?
   a. Defending against the charge of antinomianism
   b. Expanding on the doctrine of election and Israel
   c. Explaining his ministry as an Apostle to the gentiles
   d. Providing reasons for having not yet visited Rome

2. Who likely carried Paul's letter from Corinth to Rome?
   a. Aquila
   b. Junia
   c. Phoebe
   d. Prisca

3. There are almost three times as many greetings in Romans than in any other of Paul's letters.
   a. True
   b. False

4. Paul's greetings highlight the importance of women in Christian ministry.
   a. True
   b. False

5. Who is associated with the word "apostle" in Paul's greetings?
   a. Aquila
   b. Junia
   c. Phoebe
   d. Prisca

6. What attribute of God does Paul end Romans with as an encouragement?
   a. God's omnipresence
   b. God's omnipotence
   c. God's sovereignty
   d. God's wisdom

Answer Key—Paul's Conclusion

REFLECTION & DISCUSSION QUESTIONS

Before the Video

What Do You Think?

These are personal questions. The answers should be based on your own knowledge and experience.

Scripture Reading

- How was the "mystery" of God revealed?

  The "mystery hidden for ages in God" has been revealed in many ways. Chiefly, it was "realized in Christ," but it is also seen "through the church." Paul himself sees his Apostleship as another way that this mystery has been revealed in his preaching to the gentiles and been instrumental in bringing "to light" God's plan so that others may understand.

During the Video

Major Themes

- How does Paul reemphasize to the Romans that he is not antinomian in his teaching?

  In Romans 1:5, Paul declares that he preaches the "obedience of faith," holding faith and obedience together. Again, in Romans 15:18, Paul says, "For I will not venture to speak of anything except what Christ has accomplished through me to bring the Gentiles to obedience—by word and deed." Paul affirms both the free grace of God and the importance of holiness. There is nothing antinomian or legalistic in his teaching.

- What reasons does Paul give for not having yet visited the church in Rome? Why is he eager to visit soon?

  One of the reasons that Paul had not yet visited the church in Rome at the time of his writing was that he was busy planting and ministering to churches elsewhere. His desire was to preach where Christ was not yet known instead of building on someone else's foundation (Rom. 15:20). Since Paul's ministry to the gentiles in the regions where he was already at work had been successful, he desired to go beyond Rome to Spain. Paul's eagerness to visit Rome was also strategic for the advance of the gospel.

Phoebe and Junia

- How does Paul describe Phoebe? Did she hold this office in the church?

  Paul names Phoebe as "a servant of the church at Cenchreae" (Rom. 16:1). The word for "servant" used in this passage is the same word for "deacon" (diakonon). *One thing we must bear in mind is that this word has been used throughout Paul's letter to the Romans and never in the technical sense of referring to the office of deacon. It is always used in the more general sense of "servant," one who has given his or her life for the ministry of the church.*

- How does Paul describe Junia? Did she hold this office in the church?

  In Romans 16:7, Paul greets Andronicus and Junia, who are "well known to the apostles." Many scholars believe that another accurate translation of this phrase would be "well known among the apostles." Even if this is granted, just as Paul was not using the word "deacon" in a technical sense in Romans 16:1, it is most likely the case that he isn't using the word "apostle" to refer to the church office, but rather in a broader sense as someone "sent out."

Final Blessings

- How does Paul end his final instruction to the Romans for unity in confidence and hope?

  Paul begins a final appeal to the Romans in 16:17, calling them to watchfulness for the sake of unity. This includes watching out for people who create divisions in the church. The Romans, whose "obedience is known to all" (v. 19), are rather to be innocent in such things. Paul concludes confidently that "the God of peace will soon crush Satan under your feet" (v. 20), looking forward to the final judgment of God and giving us a glimpse of the narrative arc of redemptive history, extending all the way back to the first promise in the garden to the serpent's final demise (see Gen. 3:15).

- How can "the only wise God" (Rom. 16:27) be thought of as Paul's parting encouragement to the Romans and to us?

  Paul's letter to the Romans is tightly composed, and he never loses hold of his main themes or reasons for writing the letter. It may seem that the choice to call God "the only wise God" is insignificant, but it is a powerful word about God if traced through Paul's letter. Consider the doxology of Romans 11:33–36 or the folly of foolishness that was described in Romans 1:22. We need the wisdom of God in the Christian life, so in calling God "the only wise God," perhaps Paul has given us a parting encouragement to live according to His wisdom.

After the Video

- How might Paul have impressed upon the Romans their need to be concerned for poor and suffering Christians? How ought we to minister to such Christians?

  The Romans had a deep concern for Jewish Christians, and Paul corrects them concerning some matters related to this in his letter. In Romans 15, Paul talks about his plans to bring an offering for the poor in the Jerusalem church, naming a number of congregations or regional churches that had contributed to this offering. Dr. Godfrey speculated that perhaps Paul is making the Romans consider the question "Where is our offering for those in Jerusalem?" This should also make us ask, "How should we be taking care of poor and suffering Christians?" Supplying for their needs is essential, and Paul's call for prayer for his trip to Jerusalem helps us identify prayer as something that is also indispensable.

- Why might Paul's personal greeting to the Romans be so extensive?

  More than in any other letter, Paul in Romans extends greetings to individual after individual. One of the complaints that the Romans may have had concerning Paul was his not yet visiting them. While Rome was a capital city and many people from other churches may have moved there, Paul also communicates something else in his long greeting: he knows the church better than they might think. This is perhaps why Paul has insights into what is being said about him in the church. Paul has a depth of knowledge about the people of the Roman church and deep ties of friendship that defy the accusations that he has neglected them.

- As you reflect on your experience in studying Paul's letter to the Romans in this teaching series, what concepts, verses, or passages have most significantly shaped your understanding of this letter?

  These questions are personal. Your answer should reflect on the main ideas expressed in this teaching series and include a description of how your own understanding of Romans has changed or deepened as a result.

REVIEW QUIZ

1. **B.**
   Paul revisits a number of the major themes that we have seen throughout his letter. He speaks of the gospel and its going forth to the gentiles, defending his calling as Apostle to the gentiles. He highlights his teaching of the obedience of faith against any accusations of antinomianism. He also addresses the reasons that he has not visited Rome, which he first brought up in Romans 1:8–15.

2. **C.**
   Paul was in the area of Corinth when he wrote his letter to the Romans. He mentions Phoebe first in his personal greetings, commending her to the Romans as "a servant of the church at Cenchreae," a church also in the area of Corinth. She was likely the carrier of Paul's letter.

3. **A.**
   Paul mentions at least twenty-eight people in concluding his letter to the Romans. In his letter to the Colossians, Paul names about ten people (the second-most number of names mentioned at the end of Paul's letters).

4. **A.**

   Women were very important to Paul's ministry and are essential to the ministry of the church. This is seen in Paul's commendations and greetings at the end of his letter to the Romans. Eight or nine of the twenty-eight people named in his letter are women.

5. **B.**

   In Romans 16:7, Paul says: "Greet Andronicus and Junia, my kinsmen and my fellow prisoners. They are well known to the apostles, and they were in Christ before me." Some believe that "well known to the apostles" can be translated "well known among the apostles."

6. **D.**

   We need God's wisdom in the Christian life, and Paul ends his letter by praising "the only wise God" (Rom. 16:27). Paul also praised God for His wisdom in his doxology in Romans 11:33–36.